AWA UPSH

PRESENTS

CASUAL

JASON STARR
Writer

DALIBOR TALAJIĆ
Artist

MARCO LESKO
Colorist

STEVE WANDS
Letterer

DANI
Cover Artist

BRAD SIMPSON
Cover Colorist

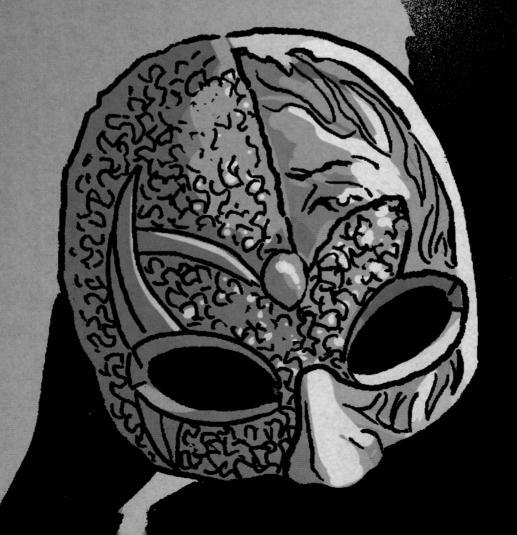

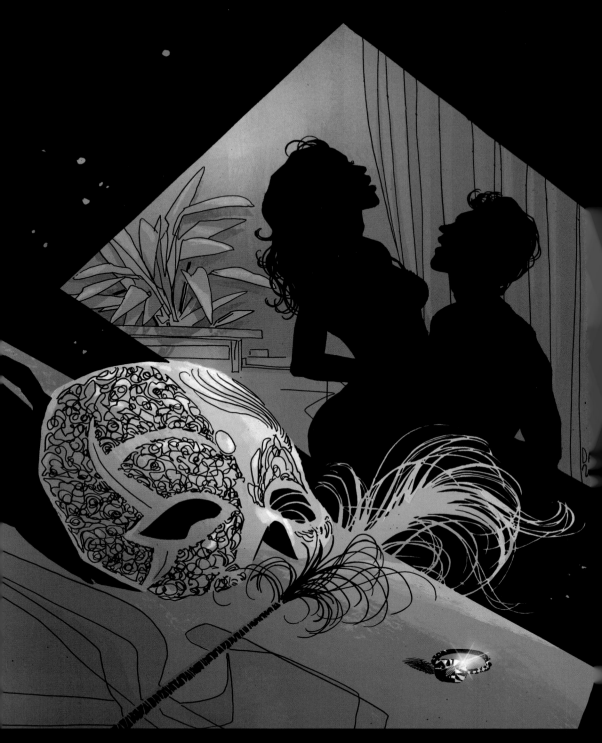

 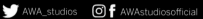 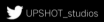 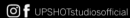

AWA UPSHOT   AWA_studios   AWAstudiosofficial   UPSHOT_studios   UPSHOTstudiosofficial

Axel Alonso Chief Creative Officer
Ariane Baya Accounting Associate
Chris Burns Production Editor
Ramsee Chand AWA Studios Assistant
Thea Cheuk Assistant Editor
Stan Chou Art Director & Logo Designer
Michael Coast Senior Editor
Jaime Coyne Associate Editor
Frank Fochetta Senior Consultant, Sales & Distribution
William Graves Managing Editor

Bill Jemas CEO & Publisher
Jackie Liu Digital Marketing Manager
Bosung Kim Graphic Designer
Allison Mase Project Manager
Dulce Montoya Associate Editor
Kevin Park Associate General Counsel
Daphney Stephan Accounting Assistant
Zach Studin President, AWA Studios
Harry Sweezey Finance Associate
Lisa Y. Wu Marketing Manager

ANHATTAN
WHAT'S BURNING?
I ALWAYS FORGET HOW HOT THIS THING GETS.
JUSTIN, QUIET!
WAH AHA AHA!
THE FLAME'S TOO HIGH.
IF I HAVE IT TOO LOW, THEY FALL APART. IF I HAVE IT TOO HIGH, THEY BURN.
I CAN'T WIN.
AHA AHA WHAHHH!
ANOTHER MULLIGAN.
HE DROPPED HIS BOTTLE.
YOU DIDN'T WIPE IT FIRST?
IT ISN'T DIRTY.
I'M STARVING, WHEN'S BREAKFAST GONNA BE DONE?
BEEP BEEP BEEP
YOU GOTTA BE KIDDIN' ME.

BEEP BEEP BEEP
THE ALARM'S TOO CLOSE TO THE STOVE. THE DESIGN OF THIS APARTMENT SUCKS.
MAKE IT STOP. MAKE IT *STOP.*
I HAVE TO RUN. NEW CLIENTS ARE IN FROM OUT OF TOWN AND I'M ALREADY RUNNING LATE.
AT LEAST YOU GET TO ESCAPE THE MADNESS FOR A WHILE.
I'LL MAKE IT UP TO YOU, I PROMISE.
NO WORRIES. WE'LL SEE YOU AT SEVEN.
WHAT'S AT SEVEN?
I ARRANGED A SITTER FOR JUSTIN.
I ASKED YOU TO PLEASE ENTER EVENTS DIRECTLY INTO MY CALENDAR.
SORRY, MUST'VE BEEN A LITTLE BUSY THAT DAY.
YOU'RE GONNA COME, RIGHT MOMMY?
OF COURSE I'LL BE THERE, SWEETIE.
SORRY, I LOVE YOU.
LOVE YOU TOO.

HOW LONG HAVE YOU HAD THIS SPACE?
THE FIRM'S BEEN HERE FOR GOING ON FOUR YEARS. BEFORE THAT WE WERE DOWNTOWN IN THE FINANCIAL DISTRICT.
AND HOW LONG HAVE YOU BEEN A PARTNER?
ABOUT SEVEN YEARS.
WE'RE VERY EXCITED TO BE WORKING WITH YOU. AND WE'RE EXCITED ABOUT THE FUTURE.
LIKEWISE. I'M SURE WE'LL FIND MANY OPPORTUNITIES TO HELP YOU EXPAND IN NEW YORK CITY.
THAT SOUNDS FANTASTIC.
ANGELA FOLEY, HARRISON WEXLER, MICHAEL STERN, MEET MY CO-PARTNERS DENISE JENKINS AND JAMES STEVENSON.
PLEASURE TO MEET YOU.
YES, IT'S GREAT TO HAVE YOU ALL IN TOWN AND ON BOARD. HOPE THE CITY'S BEEN TREATING YOU WELL SO FAR.
SO FAR I'VE ONLY SEEN THE INSIDE OF MY HOTEL ROOM, BUT THE VIEW'S GREAT AND I CAN SEE THE PARK AND THE RIVER.
WE'LL SHOW YOU AROUND A BIT, DON'T WORRY.
BZZZT BZZZT
EXCUSE ME, ONE SECOND.

EVERYTHING OKAY?
NO, EVERYTHING'S OFFICIALLY NOT OKAY. WHERE ARE JUSTIN'S DIAPERS?
WHAHHHH! WHAHHHH!
I CAN'T TALK ABOUT THIS RIGHT NOW. I'M IN THE MIDDLE OF A VERY IMPORTANT MEETING.
WELL, I'M IN THE MIDDLE OF TRYING TO GET POOP OFF MY JACKET IN FRONT OF EMILY'S SCHOOL. TALK ABOUT A TOTAL SHIT SHOW. WHY IS THE DIAPER BAG EMPTY?
WHA, AHHA, WHAAA!
YOU TOLD ME YOU PUT MORE DIAPERS IN--
TAP
SO SORRY ABOUT THAT.

HOW DOES THE REST OF YOUR DAY LOOK?
WE HAVE MEETINGS MOST OF THE DAY, AND THEN WE'RE HAVING A LITTLE SOIRÉE AT HUDSON YARDS LATER. WOULD BE GREAT IF YOU COULD JOIN.
WISH I COULD, BUT I HAVE TO GET BACK TO CONNECTICUT.
I CAN'T MAKE IT EITHER. HOW ABOUT YOU, JENNIFER?
UM...YES, SURE. THAT SOUNDS TERRIFIC.
UR NEW YORK OFFICES VILL BE THE JEWEL OF OUR CORPORATION..."
...AND IT'S ONLY THE BEGINNING. OVER THE NEXT YEAR WE'LL BE EXPANDING TO PARIS, BERLIN, COPENHAGEN, ROME...
WE CERTAINLY HOPE TO BE THERE WITH YOU EVERY STEP OF THE WAY.
DID I HEAR YOU MENTION ROME?

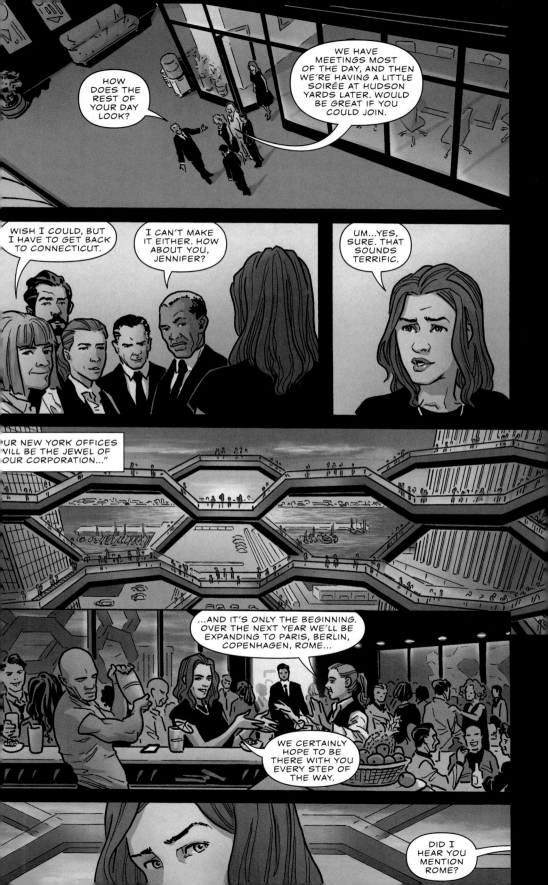

HI, ALEX, I'M SO GLAD YOU COULD MAKE IT.
MY DINNER PLANS WERE PUSHED BACK, SO I WAS ABLE TO SQUEEZE IT IN.
ALEX MILES, MEET JENNIFER RYAN, ONE OF OUR BRILLIANT NEW ATTORNEYS. ALEX IS ONE OF OUR MAJOR NEW INVESTORS. HE'S IN TOWN THIS WEEK FROM CALIFORNIA.
PLEASURE.
NICE TO MEET YOU.
I WAS RECENTLY IN ITALY FOR TWO WEEKS. MAINLY BUSINESS, BUT I WAS ABLE TO TRAVEL.
ROME, FLORENCE, BUT ALSO GOT TO THE AMALFI COAST. VIETRI SUL MARE WAS SPECTACULAR.
LUCKY YOU, I HAVEN'T BEEN TO ITALY IN AGES.
WHERE HAVE I SEEN YOU BEFORE?
UM, I'M NOT SURE.
I KNOW... AN ACTRESS IN A STREET CAR REVIVAL I SAW LAST YEAR. YOU HAVE A DOPPLEGANGER OFF-BROADWAY.
WAS MY DOPPLE-GANGER BLANCHE OR STELLA?
BLANCHE, OF COURSE.
HA, I HAVE PULLED IN MY SHARE OF BAD BOYS.
EXCUSE ME.

NEW CHEF THERE [...]CREDIBLE, BUT IT [...]ES *WEEKS* TO [...]ET A TABLE.
PERSONALLY, I DON'T MIND EATING AT THE BAR BUT--
I *LOVE* EATING AT THE BAR. IT FEELS SO--
EUROPEAN.
EXACTLY.
NO ONE ACTUALLY LIKES FRENCH REDS MORE THAN ITALIAN REDS.
THEY JUST SAY THAT BECAUSE THAT'S WHAT THEY *THINK* THEY'RE SUPPOSED TO SAY.
I'M NOT CONVINCED THAT YOU'VE HAD THE BEST FRENCH REDS THERE ARE.
WELL WHEN YOU SIT AT THE BAR YOU GET TO KNOW YOUR WINES PRETTY WELL.
I *NEED* TO [...]RAVEL. IT KEEPS ME OPEN-MINDED.
I WISH I COULD TRAVEL MORE, BUT WITH TWO KIDS...IT WAS SO MUCH EASIER WHEN ALL I HAD TO CARRY WAS A BACKPACK.
YEAH, I GET THAT.
ARE YOU CLOSE WITH YOUR FAMILY?
MY PARENTS WERE GREAT, BUT THEY WORKED SO MUCH THAT I NEVER SAW THEM. THAT CAN GET LONELY FOR A SHY KID.
I WAS SHY TOO.
REALLY? BUT YOU'RE SO BOLD.
KUNDERA'S EQUATING IT WITH FREEDOM. THINK ABOUT THE CONTEXT OF WHEN THE BOOK WAS WRITTEN.
THAT MAY BE THE INTENT BUT IT'S NOT THE *MESSAGE.* GRANTED, IT'S BEEN YEARS SINCE I READ IT AND I WAS IN A VERY DIFFERENT PLACE IN MY LIFE, BUT IT SEEMS TO ME THAT IT'S NOT SO MUCH FREEDOM AS CONFINEMENT.
EVERY TIME. OXFORD COMMA EVERY TIME.
BUT YOU DON'T NEED IT EVERY TIME.
I AM A LAWYER AND AS A LAWYER I REQUIRE PRECISION. SO, YES. I NEED TO USE IT. EVERY. TIME.

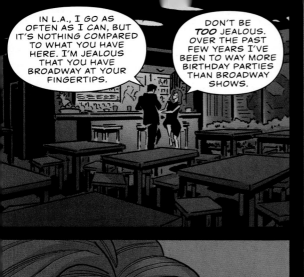

IN L.A., I GO AS OFTEN AS I CAN, BUT IT'S NOTHING COMPARED TO WHAT YOU HAVE HERE. I'M JEALOUS THAT YOU HAVE BROADWAY AT YOUR FINGERTIPS.

DON'T BE *TOO* JEALOUS. OVER THE PAST FEW YEARS I'VE BEEN TO WAY MORE BIRTHDAY PARTIES THAN BROADWAY SHOWS.

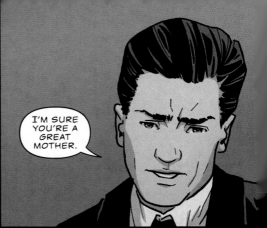

I'M SURE YOU'RE A GREAT MOTHER.

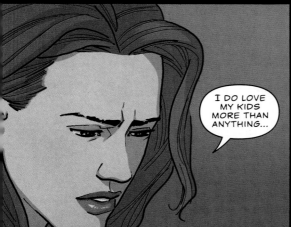

I DO LOVE MY KIDS MORE THAN ANYTHING...

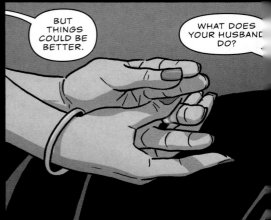

BUT THINGS COULD BE BETTER.

WHAT DOES YOUR HUSBAND DO?

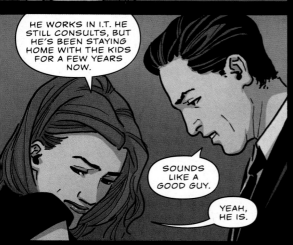

HE WORKS IN I.T. HE STILL CONSULTS, BUT HE'S BEEN STAYING HOME WITH THE KIDS FOR A FEW YEARS NOW.

SOUNDS LIKE A GOOD GUY.

YEAH, HE IS.

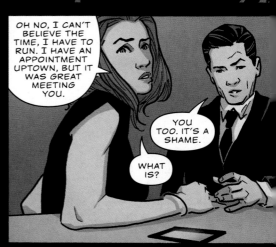

OH NO, I CAN'T BELIEVE THE TIME, I HAVE TO RUN. I HAVE AN APPOINTMENT UPTOWN, BUT IT WAS GREAT MEETING YOU.

YOU TOO. IT'S A SHAME.

WHAT IS?

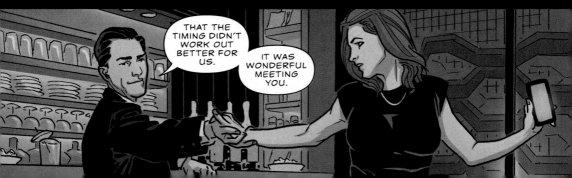

THAT THE TIMING DIDN'T WORK OUT BETTER FOR US.

IT WAS WONDERFUL MEETING YOU.

TAXI! TAXI!
CAN'T YOU TAKE THE WEST SIDE HIGHWAY?
TRAFFIC'S CRAZY. THE WHOLE CITY'S BACKED UP TONIGHT.
OKAY, WHATEVER. JUST GET THERE FAST. PLEASE.
EXCUSE ME. WHERE'RE YOU GOING?
THE RECITAL.
THE RECITAL? THAT ENDED LIKE A HALF HOUR AGO.

HEY... I'M SO, SO SORRY.
I KNOW, I GOT YOUR TEXTS. IT'S OKAY.
YOU'RE NOT UPSET?
IT IS WHAT IT IS.
I HAD TO GO TO THIS WORK THING IN HUDSON YARDS AND THE TRAFFIC WAS INSANE. I SHOULD'VE TAKEN THE SUBWAY. I ALWAYS MAKE THAT MISTAKE, TRYING TO GET THROUGH MIDTOWN AT THAT HOUR IS ALWAYS A NIGHTMARE.
WHATEVER.
HOW'S EM?
HOW DO YOU THINK? HER MOM PROMISED SHE'D BE SOMEWHERE AND DIDN'T SHOW UP. SHE WAS UPSET.
IS SHE STILL UP?
NO, SHE WAS ZONKED. PASSED RIGHT OUT. THE SITTER SAID JUSTIN FELL ASLEEP, WHICH MEANS HE'LL BE A TASMANIAN DEVIL AT FOUR A.M.
DON'T WORRY, I'LL WAKE UP WITH HIM.
SPEAKING OF ZONKED, I'M GONNA WATCH THE REST OF THE GAME IN BED AND CRASH. G'NIGHT.
GOODNIGHT.

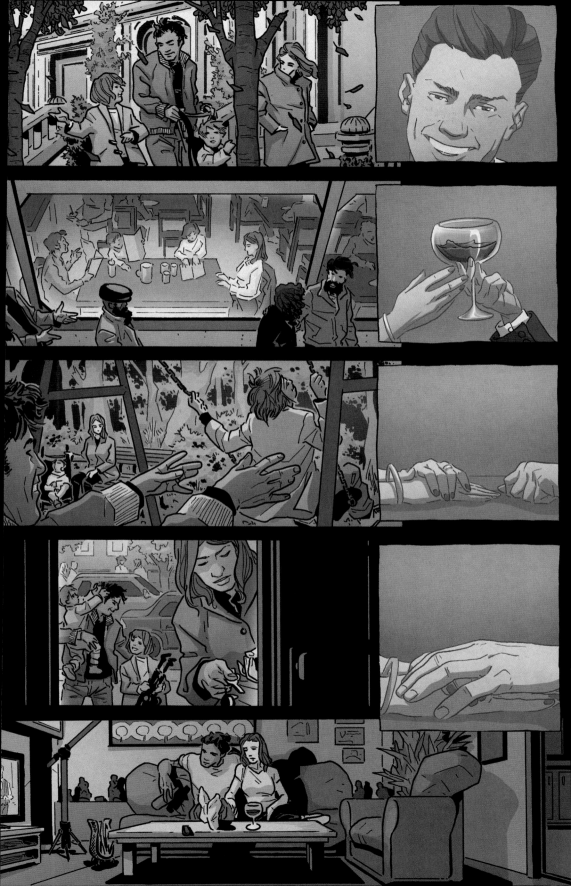

THAT'S ALL, THANK YOU.
WHY HELLO THERE, MS. DUBOIS.
OH MY GOD, ALEX, HI. WHAT'RE YOU DOING HERE?
I SHOULD ASK YOU THE SAME QUESTION.
I'M STAYING A FEW BLOCKS AWAY, AT THE ROGER SMITH. I'VE BEEN GETTING MY COFFEE HERE EVERY MORNING SINCE I'VE BEEN IN TOWN.
THAT'S HILARIOUS. MY OFFICE IS RIGHT AROUND THE CORNER. I COME HERE EVERY DAY FOR MY SECOND CUP--I ALWAYS SEEM TO HIT A WALL AT AROUND TEN.
I'M IN BETWEEN MEETINGS MYSELF. WANT TO JOIN?
I'D LOVE TO, BUT I HAVE TO GET BACK TO THE OFFICE TO FINISH A DELIVERABLE.
WHAT ARE YOU DOING LATER? AT AROUND SIX?
I PROBABLY HAVE TO STAY LATE AT WORK. WHY?
TODAY'S MY LAST DAY IN NEW YORK, I HAVE TO CATCH A FLIGHT TO L.A. IN THE MORNING. CARE TO JOIN ME FOR AN EARLY DRINK AT MY HOTEL BAR?
I'M SORRY...
...I REALLY CAN'T DO THAT. BUT IT WAS GREAT RUNNING INTO YOU AGAIN AND I HOPE YOU HAVE A SAFE TRIP BACK.
IF YOU CHANGE YOUR MIND, YOU KNOW WHERE TO FIND ME.

IT'S A MATTER OF *PRIORITIES.*
I KNOW YOU HAVE A FAMILY, YOUNG KIDS, I'VE BEEN THERE MYSELF, BUT YOU CAN'T LET IT INTERFERE WITH YOUR DAY-TO-DAY.
IT USUALLY DOESN'T.
ANGELA SAID YOU DISAPPEARED FROM THE EVENT THE OTHER NIGHT, DIDN'T EVEN SAY GOODBYE.
I KNOW, AND I EMAILED HER TO APOLOGIZE. I HAD TO GET UPTOWN FOR SOMETHING URGENT.
UNLESS SOMEONE'S DYING THE ONLY *URGENCY* IS YOUR RESPONSIBILITIES AT THIS FIRM.
YOU'RE RIGHT. BELIEVE ME, I WANTED TO STAY. I WAS ENJOYING THE EVENING VERY MUCH. I MEAN, I HAVEN'T HAD ANY SORT OF ADULT NIGHT OUT IN AGES.
THIS IS SIMPLY A MATTER OF SETTING YOUR PRIORITIES STRAIGHT, JENNIFER.
WE ALL HAVE OTHER LIVES AND I DON'T EXPECT YOURS TO REVOLVE SOLELY AROUND THIS JOB. BUT WHEN YOU'RE HERE I NEED YOU TO BE *HERE.*
I HOPE YOU CAN UNDERSTAND.

HOW WAS TODAY?
AWESOME.
JUSTIN TOOK A NORMAL NAP SO HE SHOULD GET TO SLEEP EARLY TONIGHT.
EMILY CAME BACK FROM THAT CLASS TRIP TO THE AQUARIUM AND SHE'S SO STOKED, SHE CAN'T STOP TALKING ABOUT IT.
THAT'S GREAT. SO IT'S OKAY IF I STAY A LITTLE LATE AT WORK?
YEAH, TOTALLY.
AS SOON AS JUSTIN FALLS ASLEEP, I'M GONNA BINGE SOMETHING ON NETFLIX SO TAKE YOUR TIME.
OKAY, SHOULDN'T BE TOO LATE. LOVE YOU.
LOVE YOU, TOO.
YOU MADE IT.
YES, I WAS JUST PASSING BY, SO I THOUGHT I'D STOP BY FOR A QUICK DRINK.

I'VE NEVER DONE ANYTHING LIKE THIS.
LIKE WHAT?
STEPPING OUT OF MY MARRIAGE.
DON'T WORRY...
...I'LL BE GENTLE.
WHY THE MASK?
MAYBE IT'S NOT A MASK. MAYBE IT'S THE ***REAL ME.***
IT'S JUST A LITTLE KINK. WHAT'S YOURS?
ACTUALLY, NEVER MIND.
WHY
LL, WHEN
'OU CAN
SHOW?

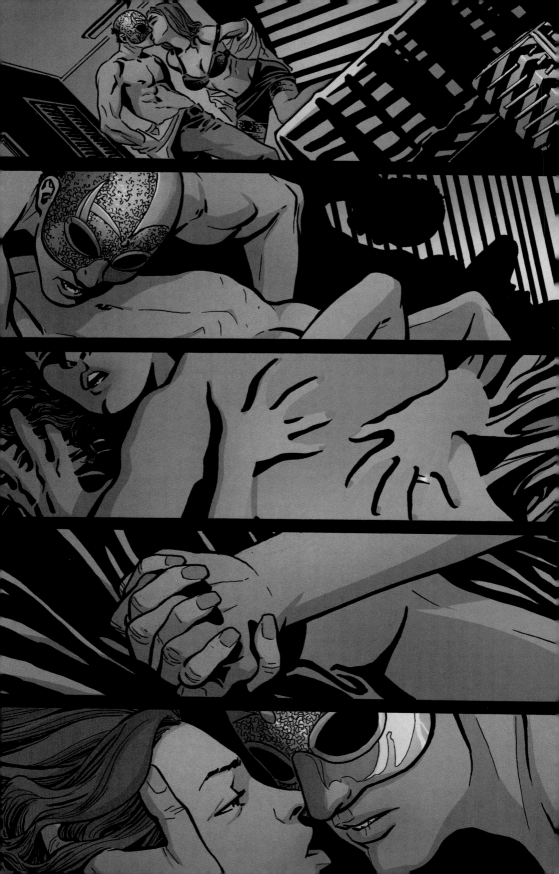

LEAVING ALREADY?
SORRY, I HAVE TO GET HOME.
YOU'RE SO GORGEOUS, STRONG, AND IN CONTROL. YOU'RE THE **REAL DEAL** JENNIFER RYAN, AREN'T YOU?
THIS WAS NICE. HAVE A GREAT TRIP BACK TO L.A.
WHEN CAN I SEE YOU AGAIN?
I'M MARRIED SO THAT DEFINITELY WOULDN'T BE A GOOD IDEA.
YOU DIDN'T EM SO MARRIED A COUPLE OF MINUTES AGO.
GOODBYE, ALEX.

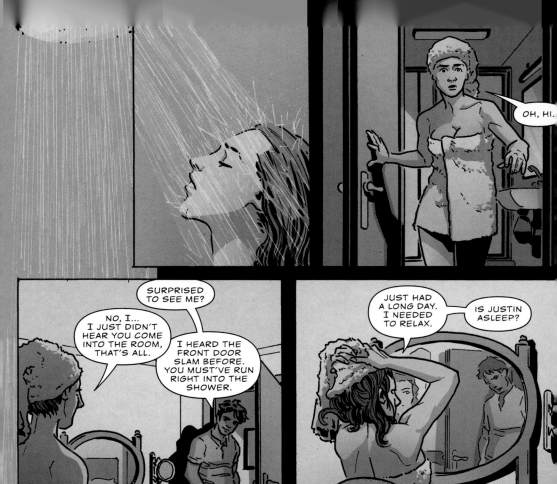

OH, HI.

SURPRISED TO SEE ME?

NO, I... I JUST DIDN'T HEAR YOU COME INTO THE ROOM, THAT'S ALL.

I HEARD THE FRONT DOOR SLAM BEFORE. YOU MUST'VE RUN RIGHT INTO THE SHOWER.

JUST HAD A LONG DAY. I NEEDED TO RELAX.

IS JUSTIN ASLEEP?

YEAH, HE'S DOWN, AND EMILY'S WAITIN' FOR YOU TO RE HER GOODNIG MOON.

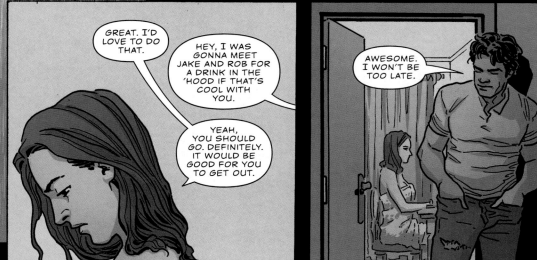

GREAT. I'D LOVE TO DO THAT.

HEY, I WAS GONNA MEET JAKE AND ROB FOR A DRINK IN THE 'HOOD IF THAT'S COOL WITH YOU.

YEAH, YOU SHOULD GO. DEFINITELY. IT WOULD BE GOOD FOR YOU TO GET OUT.

AWESOME. I WON'T BE TOO LATE.

.30 A.M.
--EEP EEEP EEEEP
I'LL GET THE KIDS READY. YOU SLEEP IN.
WHAT?... OH, 'KAY... THANKS.
CAN I HAVE SOME MORE ORANGE JUICE, MOMMY?
YES, YOU CERTAINLY CAN.
HEY THERE.
DADDY'S UP!
HEY... WOW, THANKS FOR DOING ALL OF THIS. GOT BACK A LITTLE LATER THAN I ANTICIPATED.
IT'S OKAY, YOU *DESERVE* A BREAK. HEY, YOU KNOW WHAT WOULD BE FUN? A DATE NIGHT.
I'VE BEEN SUGGESTING THAT FOREVER, BUT YOU ALWAYS HAVE TO WORK LATE.
I KNOW. BUT IT'S ABOUT *PRIORITIES,* RIGHT? AND I THINK WE NEED TO MAKE *EACH OTHER* THE PRIORITY SOMETIMES.
I'M TOTALLY UP FOR THAT.

SHAKE SHACK
...AND I HAVE A SURPRISE FOR YOU.
GRETA VAN FLEET TICKETS FOR NEXT SATURDAY NIGHT.
I'VE BEEN DYING TO SEE THEM. THIS IS SO AMAZING, BABY.
WE'LL HAVE A CHANCE TO CELEBRATE.
CELEBRATE WHAT?
I HIT A HOME RUN AT WORK. OUR NEW CLIENTS HIRED US AS THEIR CHIEF COUNSEL.
WOW, BABY, THAT'S SO AWESOME. FUCK YEAH!
DADDY JUST CURSED.
NO I DIDN'T.
YES YOU DID.
NO I DID NOT.
BZZZZ
PRIVATE NUMBER
I SHOULD TAKE THIS.

HELLO?
HEY JENNIFER, IT'S ALEX... ALEX MILES.
OH, HELLO. HOW DID YOU GET THIS NUMBER?
ANGELA GAVE IT TO ME.
I'M AT MY HOTEL. I THOUGHT YOU MIGHT WANT TO MEET UP LATER.
I THOUGHT YOU WERE BACK IN L.A.
GOOD NEWS. I DECIDED TO EXTEND MY STAY. I'LL BE IN TOWN FOR AT LEAST ANOTHER WEEK. SO HOW ABOUT TONIGHT WE PICK UP WHERE WE LEFT OFF?
TONIGHT I'M SPENDING TIME WITH MY FAMILY. I TOLD YOU I CAN'T SEE YOU AGAIN, ALEX.
I THOUGHT YOU MIGHT'VE CHANGED YOUR MIND...
WELL, I HAVEN'T, OKAY?
YOU WERE UP FRONT ABOUT YOUR SITUATION GOING IN. I RESPECT THAT ABOUT YOU. YOU'RE HONEST--NOT A LOT OF THAT GOING AROUND THESE DAYS.
YOU'RE A GREAT WOMAN, AND I HAVE SO MUCH RESPECT FOR YOU.
REALLY, JENNIFER...

...YOU HAVE NO IDEA.

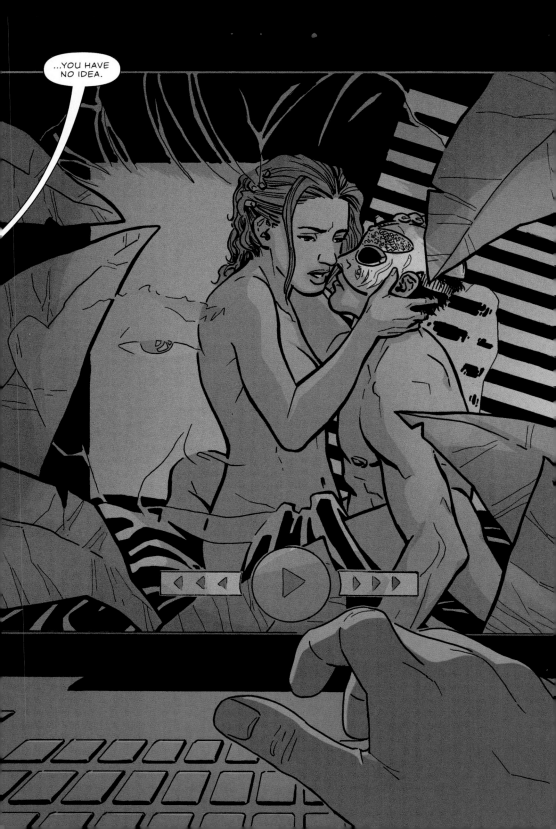

DANI
2020

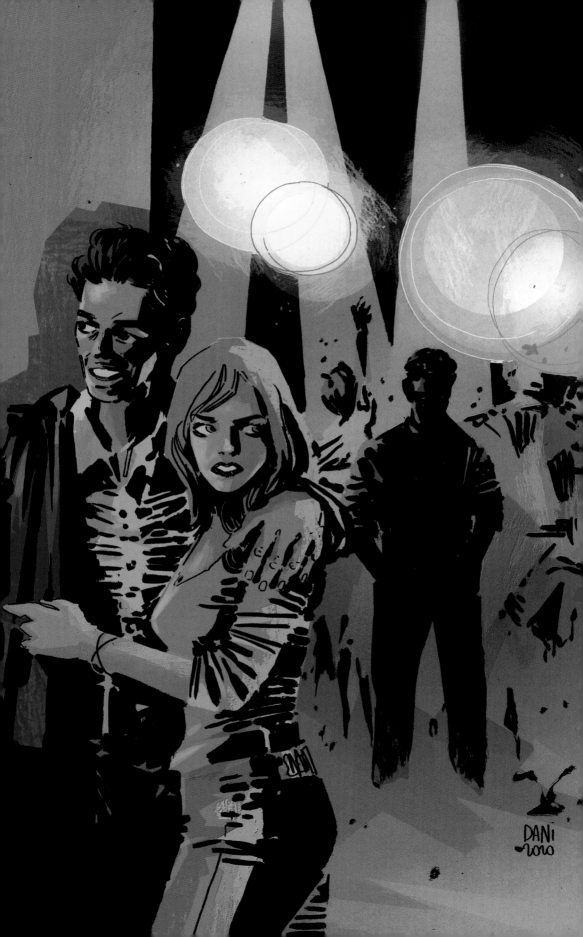

WHAT'RE YOU READING?
NOTHING FUN, UNFORTUNATELY. REVIEWING DOCS FOR WORK.
I SHOULD START READING AGAIN. I CAN'T REMEMBER THE LAST TIME I READ A BOOK.
MAYBE IT'S HANGING OUT WITH THE KIDS ALL DAY, OR I'M ON MY PHONE TOO MUCH, BUT MY ATTENTION SPAN'S **FUCKED.**
YOU SMELL GOOD.
I **DO?**
YOU **ALWAYS** SMELL AMAZING.
MM, THIS IS **MUCH** NICER THAN READING THOSE DOCS.
DAMN RIGHT IT IS.
BZZZ BZZZ
WHO IS IT?

NO ONE.
I can't stop thinking about you, Jennifer. Is the feeling mutual?
message
...JUST WORK.
COOL.
EVERYTHING OKAY?
YEAH, FINE, I JUST HAD A STRESSFUL DAY. WORK PRESSURE, YOU KNOW? YOU JUST FINISH.
YOU SURE?
YEAH, GO 'HEAD.
MM, THIS FEELS SO NICE.

WE'LL HAVE TO REEVALUATE THE PROBATE SITUATION, OF COURSE, BUT I'M SURE WE CAN COME UP WITH A COST-EFFECTIVE SOLUTION.
I'M SURE TOO, AND AFTER THE CLOSING ON THE HOUSTON LOCATION, WE'LL HAVE A MUCH CLEARER PICTURE OVERALL.
I HAVE A REZ FOR LUNCH AT PER SE. LIKE TO JOIN?
AW, WISH I COULD, BUT I HAVE THAT ONE O'CLOCK AND NEED TO PREP. BUT I'LL CHECK IN WITH YOU AFTER AND WE CAN GO OVER THOSE NUMBERS AGAIN.
SOUNDS GREAT...OH, I MEANT TO ASK YOU SOMETHING.
THE OTHER NIGHT AT THE COCKTAIL PARTY. THE MAN YOU INTRODUCED ME TO, ALEX MILES-- HE'S ONE OF YOUR INVESTORS?
WELL, NO TECHNICA
HE'S IN BUSINESS WITH ANOTHER CLIENT OF OURS. IT SEEMED LIKE YOU TWO WERE HAVING AN ENGROSSING CONVERSATION.
YES, HE DEFINITELY INTEREST GUY.
THAT'S RIGHT, HE SAID YOU WERE RUSHING OUT, BUT MEANT TO GIVE HIM YOUR NUMBER SO I PASSED YOURS ALONG. I ASSUMED THAT SINCE YOU WERE TALKING FOR SO LONG THAT IT WAS OKAY.
YES, OF COURSE...
...IT'S TOTALLY FINE. WE HAD AN, UM, PROJECT HE WANTED TO DISCUSS.
GREAT. IT ALWAYS FEELS GOOD TO CONNECT PEOPLE. HOPE THAT WORKS OUT FOR YOU.
SO DO I.

SHIT.
PRIVATE NUMBER
IT'S A BIG STEP IN THE RIGHT DIRECTION.
THE BEST WE CAN HOPE FOR AT THIS STAGE.
AND I THINK IT'S JUST THE BEGINNING. IF WE CAN KEEP--
THE PHEASANT AND BLACK WINTER TRUFFLE IS FANTASTIC TODAY.

ALEX... WHAT'RE YOU DOING IN THIS AREA?
JUST FINISHED UP A WORK LUNCH WITH A CLIENT. I SAID TO MYSELF, COULD THAT REALLY BE JENNIFER RYAN?
I MEAN, WHAT'RE THE ODDS, RIGHT?
I'M SORRY, THIS IS ALEX...ALEX MILES.
ALEX IS--
HOW ARE YOU?
AN OLD FRIEND. HOW LONG HAS IT BEEN?
I DON'T KNOW. HOW LONG?
TOO LONG. YOU LOOK FANTASTIC, I MUST SAY. HOW'VE YOU BEEN?
GREAT ACTUALLY, BUT WE'RE IN THE MIDDLE OF A--
OH, OF COURSE, I DON'T WANT TO INTERRUPT.
DON'T BE A STRANGER. WE SHOULD REALLY GET TOGETHER SOMETIME SOON. HAVE DRINKS, OR EVEN DINNER. WE HAVE A LOT TO CATCH UP ABOUT.
IT WAS GREAT MEETING YOU.
AND IF YOU WANT TO TRY A DESSERT, THE MARQUISE AU CHOCOLAT IS DELECTABLE.
THANK YOU FOR THE RECOMMENDATIONS.
YOU'RE VERY WELCOM
SUCH A NICE MAN.

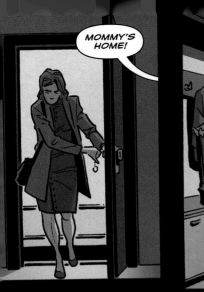

MOMMY'S HOME!

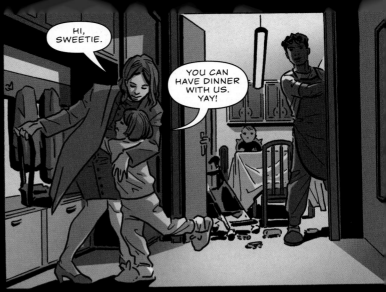

HI, SWEETIE.

YOU CAN HAVE DINNER WITH US. YAY!

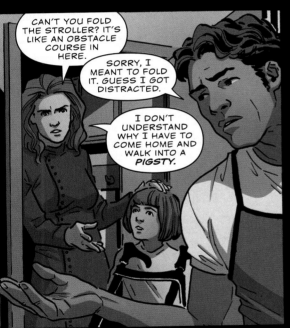

CAN'T YOU FOLD THE STROLLER? IT'S LIKE AN OBSTACLE COURSE IN HERE.

SORRY, I MEANT TO FOLD IT. GUESS I GOT DISTRACTED.

I DON'T UNDERSTAND WHY I HAVE TO COME HOME AND WALK INTO A *PIGSTY.*

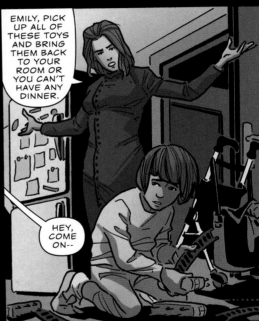

EMILY, PICK UP ALL OF THESE TOYS AND BRING THEM BACK TO YOUR ROOM OR YOU CAN'T HAVE ANY DINNER.

HEY, COME ON--

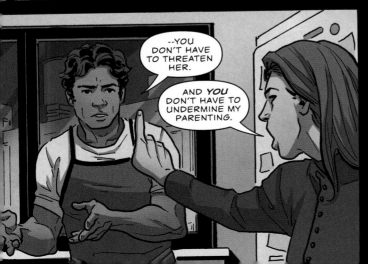

--YOU DON'T HAVE TO THREATEN HER.

AND *YOU* DON'T HAVE TO UNDERMINE MY PARENTING.

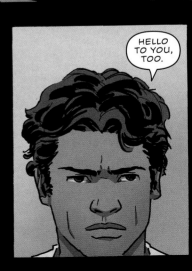

HELLO TO YOU, TOO.

HEY.
HEY.
IS THERE SOMETHING YOU WANT TO TALK ABOUT? BECAUSE WE CAN'T GO ON LIKE THIS. IT'S HARD ENOUGH WITH EVERYTHING I DO DURING THE DAY. AT NIGHT I JUST WANT PEACE.
I'M SORRY.
I DIDN'T MEAN TO TAKE MY DAY OUT ON YOU. I HAVE TO STOP DOING THAT.
YEAH, YOU DO.
I DON'T KNOW WHAT'S GOING ON. IF IT'S JUST WORK STRESS, I GET IT, BUT YOU HAVE TO LET ME IN. IF YOU WANT TO GO TO COUNSELING I'M UP FOR THAT.
I JUST VANT THINGS O BE...I DON'T NOW...STABLE WITH US. IF THAT MAKES ANY SENSE.
IT DOES.
ACTUALLY, I MEANT TO TELL YOU HOW HOT YOU LOOKED IN THAT APRON.
HOT HOUSE DAD, HUH?
THE HOTTEST.
I'M SORRY AGAIN. YOU DESERVE BETTER, AND I'M REALLY LOOKING FORWARD TO OUR DATE NIGHT TOMORROW.
ME, TOO.

I'M SO PSYCHED FOR THIS. LET'S JUST HOPE WE DON'T GET AN S.O.S. FROM THE SITTER.
DON'T WORRY. MURPHY'S LAW.
WAIT, ISN'T THAT "ANYTHING THAT CAN GO WRONG, WILL"?
YEAH, BUT YOU KNOW I DON'T BELIEVE IN THAT SHIT.

SOMEONE'S HERE TO SEE YOU.
WHO?
ALEX MILES.
WHY DID YOU LET HIM IN
SHE DIDN'T.
I HOPE I'M NOT TOO EARLY FOR MY APPOINTMENT.
IS IT POSSIBLE TO SEE YOU NOW?
FOLLOW ME, PLEASE.
MY PLEASURE.

WHAT THE HELL IS **WRONG** WITH YOU?

I THINK YOU SHOULD BE ASKING YOURSELF THAT QUESTION. YOU KNOW, GHOSTING MIGHT BE **EN VOGUE** THESE DAYS, BUT IT ISN'T VERY POLITE.

I'M NOT **GHOSTING** YOU. I WAS VERY UP FRONT WITH YOU, AND I'M WARNING YOU--YOU DON'T KNOW WHO YOU'RE MESSING WITH.

REALLY?

DO YOU HAVE A SECRET IDENTITY? IS THERE ANOTHER JENNIFER RYAN BEHIND THIS PRETTY LITTLE MASK?

THIS IS THE LAST TIME I'M WARNING YOU.

IF I SEE YOU AGAIN, IF YOU KEEP STALKING ME, I'M GOING TO TAKE APPROPRIATE MEASURES, INCLUDING CONTACTING THE POLICE.

AND WHAT WILL YOU TELL THEM?

THAT I COINCIDENTALLY RAN INTO YOU AT A RESTAURANT I FREQUENT, OR SAW YOU AND YOUR HUSBAND AT A WIDELY-ATTENDED ROCK CONCERT?

BY THE WAY, YOU MUST FIND ME INCREDIBLY ATTRACTIVE. I MEAN, TO RISK LOSING YOUR HUSBAND, **AND** YOUR TWO ADORABLE CHILDREN. IT'S VERY FLATTERING.

IF YOU COME ANYWHERE NEAR MY KIDS, I SWEAR TO FUCKING GOD, I'LL KILL YOU.

NOW **THERE'S** THE FEISTY WOMAN I REMEMBER. I KNEW SHE WAS STILL IN THERE SOMEWHERE.

BY THE WAY, I HAVE A LITTLE SURPRISE FOR YOU.

YOU'LL WANT TO CHECK YOUR EMAIL ASAP.

FUCK.
TAXI! TAXI!
GODDAMNIT.

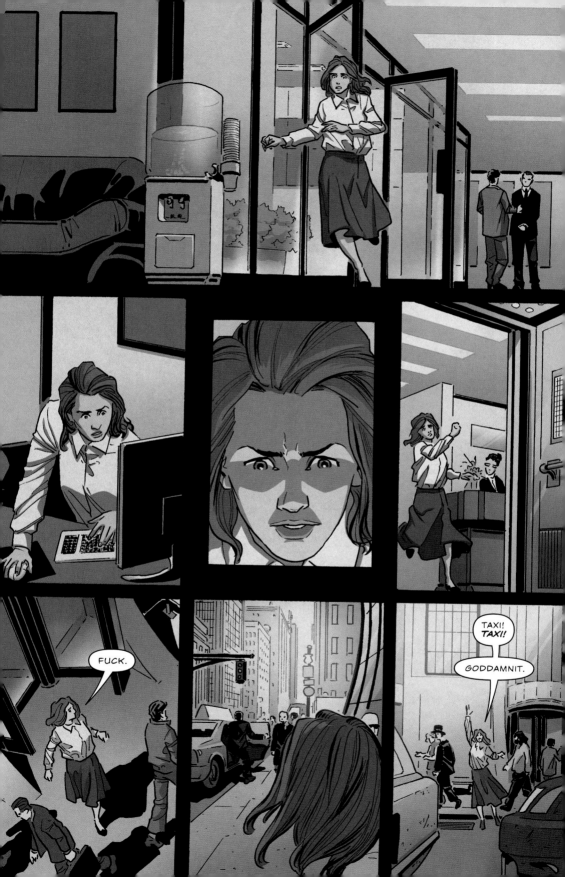

Alex Miles inves
YOU'RE FUCKING KIDDING ME.
BZZZZ
PRIVATE NUMBER
JESUS CHRIST.
I THINK I'M COMING DOWN WITH SOMETHING. I'M GOING TO HAVE TO WORK FROM HOME THE REST OF THE DAY.
OKAY...
...HOPE YOU FEEL BETTER.

HEY.
YOU WALKED RIGHT BY US. WHAT'RE YOU DOING HOME FROM WORK?
SOMETHING HAPPENED.
WHAT IS IT?
CAN WE TALK ABOUT IT UPSTAIRS?
SURE, OKAY.
WHAT'S GOING ON? YOU'RE SCARING THE SHIT OUT OF ME.
CAN YOU JUST...CAN YOU JUST PUT JUSTIN DOWN IN HIS CRIB?
OK, WHAT'S GOING ON? WHAT'S *WRONG?*
I HAVE A *CONFESSION* TO MAKE.
I KNOW YOU MIGHT NOT FORGIVE ME, BUT I HOPE YOU AT LEAST TRY.

I CHEATED ON YOU, MATTHEW. IT WAS JUST ONE TIME, A CASUAL FLING, IT MEANT NOTHING TO ME, BUT...BUT THINGS GOT COMPLICATED.
WAIT. *WHAT?*
I...I THOUGHT YOU WERE GONNA TELL ME YOU WERE SICK, OR SOMEONE DIED, BUT I DIDN'T EXPECT *THIS.*
I'M SO, SO SORRY.
I CAN'T...I CAN'T BELIEVE THIS IS HAPPENING.
I DON'T KNOW WHAT TO DO.
THIS GUY'S GETTING OBSESSIVE. I DON'T KNOW IF HE'S ACTUALLY DANGEROUS, BUT HE FOLLOWED US TO THE CONCERT LAST NIGHT... I THINK HE MIGHT BE STALKING ME.
STALKING YOU?
AND HE HAS A *VIDEO.*
HE VIDEO'D US... IN THE HOTEL ROOM. HE SAID HE WANTS MONEY-- FIFTY THOUSAND DOLLARS *IN BITCOIN*--OR HE'S GOING TO POST IT ONLINE.
HY'RE YOU ELLING ME THIS?
I...I *HAD* TO TELL YOU.
WHY? BECAUSE YOU'RE BEING *BLACKMAILED?* IF THIS GUY WASN'T BLACKMAILING YOU, YOU'D NEVER TELL ME, WOULD YOU? YOU'D JUST KEEP TELLING ME THAT "WORK'S BEEN CRAZY LATELY," AND ALL THAT OTHER BULLSHIT.
THE LAST THING I WANT IS TO HURT YOU.
WELL, YOU'VE DONE A GREAT JOB OF *THAT.*

I KNOW I FUCKED UP, DESERVE EVERYTHING I GET. ALL I CARE ABOUT IS YOU AND THE KIDS.
THE *KIDS?*
THIS GUY KNOWS ABOUT OUR *KIDS?*
YES.
FOR FUCK'S SAKE, JENNIFER, WHAT THE HELL'S *WRONG* WITH YOU?
AND YOU SAY YOU *CARE* ABOUT US? YEAH, RIGHT. HOW CAN YOU BE SO GODDAMN SELFISH?
I MADE A MISTAKE, BUT I WON'T LET ANYTHING HAPPEN, I PROMISE.
I DON'T THINK HE'S A VIOLENT GUY.
YOU DON'T THINK-- *PERIOD.*
IT'S NOT THE MONEY HE WANTS. I THINK HE'S JUST TRYING TO SCARE ME. HE GETS OFF ON POWER, CONTROL, *FEAR.*
I REALLY DON'T GIVE A SHIT HOW YOUR LOVER GETS OFF.
YOU GOT YOURSELF INTO THIS MESS, GET YOURSELF OUT OF IT.
I'M TAKING THE KIDS TO MY PARENTS, AND DON'T TRY TO STOP ME.
YOU'RE ON YOUR OWN.

SO LEMME GET THIS STRAIGHT...
YOU MEET A GUY AT A PARTY, HOOK UP IN A HOTEL ROOM, AND NOW HE'S BLACKMAILING YOU WITH A SEX TAPE?
YOU HAVE NO IDEA HOW HUMILIATING IT IS FOR ME TO BE HERE RIGHT NOW.
WHAT EXACTLY DID THIS BLACK-MAIL NOTE SAY?
HI MS. DUBOIS--THAT'S AN INSIDE REFERENCE--SEND FIFTY THOUSAND DOLLARS IN BITCOIN BY MIDNIGHT TOMORROW OR I'LL POST YOUR DEBUT VIDEO EVERYWHERE--WITH "EVERY-WHERE" IN CAPS... HE INCLUDES A QR CODE BUT I KNOW THOSE ARE ANONYMOUS AND PROBABLY CAN'T HELP YOU--
SO WHAT EXACTLY DO YOU WANT ME TO DO?
WHAT DO YOU THINK? I WANT YOU TO FIND THE SON OF A BITCH.
I'M A COP, NOT A PSYCHIC. YOU SAID YOU HAVE NO PHONE NUMBER, IN THE VIDEO YOU SAY HE'S WEARING A MASK SO WE CAN'T EVEN PROVE IT'S HIM. YOU DON'T EVEN KNOW HIS NAME.
YOU CAN TRACE PRIVATE NUMBERS. I KNOW IT'S POSSIBLE.
TO WHAT END? WHAT AM I GOING TO ARREST HIM FOR?
BLACKMAIL... STALKING.
CAN YOU PROVE HE'S STALKING YOU?
THIS IS MY LIFE, DETECTIVE RAMIREZ.
I KNOW I MADE A HUGE MISTAKE, I MIGHT'VE LOST MY FAMILY, AND I COULD LOSE MY CAREER, BUT I HAVE TO STOP HIM. WHAT IF IT'S NOT JUST ME? WHAT IF HE DOES IT TO SOMEONE ELSE?

LOOK, I GET IT, YOU FEEL USED, VIOLATED AND A LOT OF UNPLEASANT EMOTIONS. I FEEL SORRY FOR YOU, I REALLY DO.
I WISH I HAD TIME TO WORK ON EVERY CASE WHERE SOMEONE GETS PLAYED BY A SCAMMER, BUT YOU KNOW HOW OFTEN THIS HAPPENS?
SO THIS IS YOUR ANSWER? YOU WON'T DO ANYTHING?
YOU CAN HIRE A P.I. TO TRACK HIM DOWN, BUT HONESTLY, I DON'T KNOW WHAT GOOD IT'LL DO. CHANCES ARE WE WON'T BE ABLE TO CHARGE HIM WITH ANYTHING THAT STICKS AND THE FACT IS, WITH SCUMBAGS LIKE THESE, IF HE WANTS TO UPLOAD THAT VIDEO, HE WILL.
IT COULD BE ON ***PORNHUB*** RIGHT NOW.
I CAN'T LET THIS HAPPEN. I HAVE A HUSBAND, CHILDREN, CLIENTS.
I'LL GIVE YOU A LITTLE ADVICE.
DON'T GIVE HIM A FUCKIN' CENT. IF YOU PAY HIM, HE'LL JUST ASK FOR MORE, THEN WHEN WILL IT END? TRUST ME, YOU DON'T WANT TO GO DOWN THAT ROAD. I MEAN SERIOUSLY...
...WOULD YOU RATHER BE HUMILATED ***AND*** BROKE? OR JUST HUMILIATED?

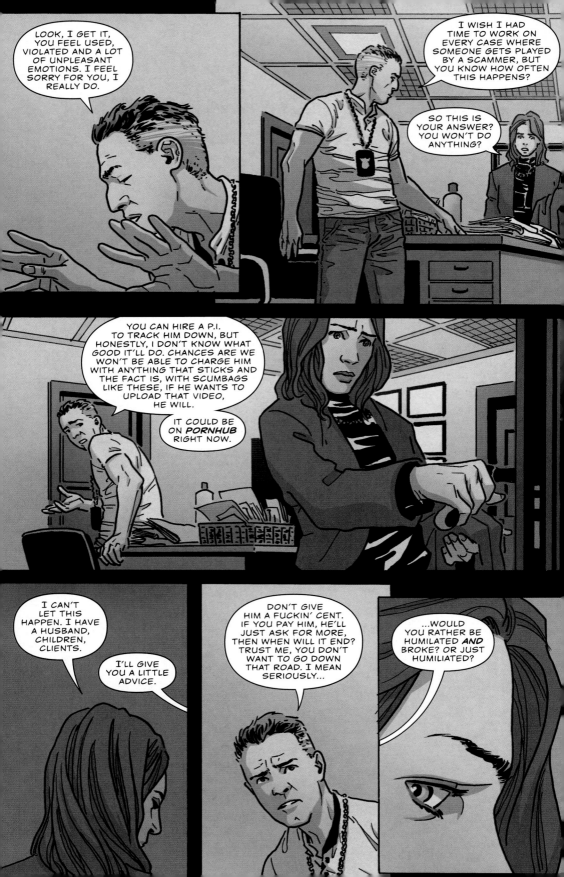

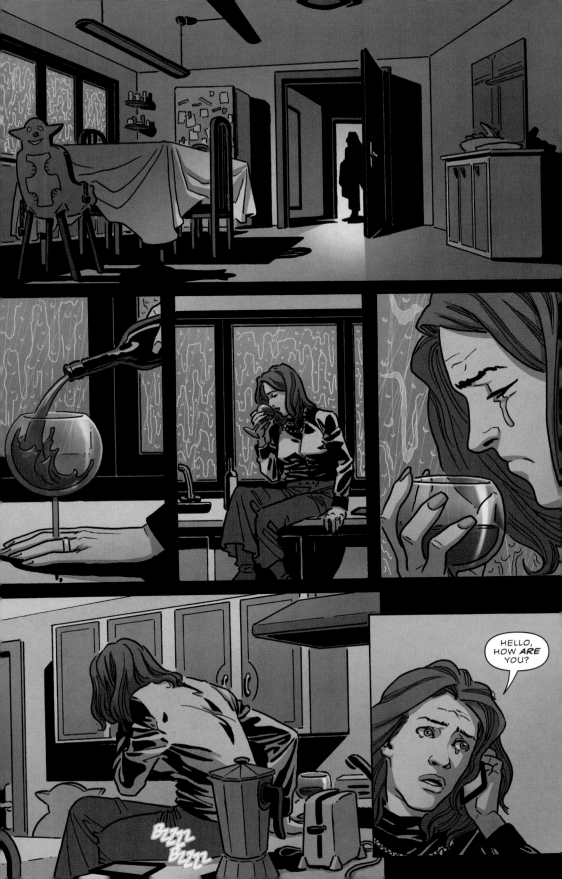

BIZZZ
BIZZZ

HELLO,
HOW ARE
YOU?

HOW'RE THE KIDS?
THEY'RE FINE. I MEAN, EMILY'S CONFUSED, SHE DOESN'T KNOW WHAT'S GOING ON, BUT SHE'S DEALING.
I'M SO SORRY, MATT.
YOU HAVE EVERY RIGHT TO HATE ME. IF YOU WANT TO TALK ABOUT IT, GO TO COUNSELING, I--
LOOK, I DON'T KNOW WHAT'S GONNA HAPPEN WITH US, I REALLY DON'T. I'M GONNA NEED TIME...A LOT OF TIME.
I UNDER-STAND...TAKE ALL THE TIME YOU WANT.
SEND ME THE VIDEO.
WHAT FOR?
I NEED TO SEE IT.
BUT IT'S... I CAN'T LET YOU SEE IT, MATTHEW. I CAN'T.
JUST SEND IT TO ME.
OKAY... OKAY.
I LOVE Y--
TAP

OU'RE
ILL UP?
YEAH, I JUST HAVE A DEADLINE ON THIS...UH... FREELANCE PROJECT.
WELL, DON'T GET TO SLEEP TOO LATE, SWEETIE. YOU'VE HAD A STRESSFUL DAY. YOU DON'T WANT TO GET SICK.
OKAY, I WON'T, MA.

OH, GOD... OH, YES.
YEAH, RIGHT THERE. LIKE THAT...LIKE THAT.

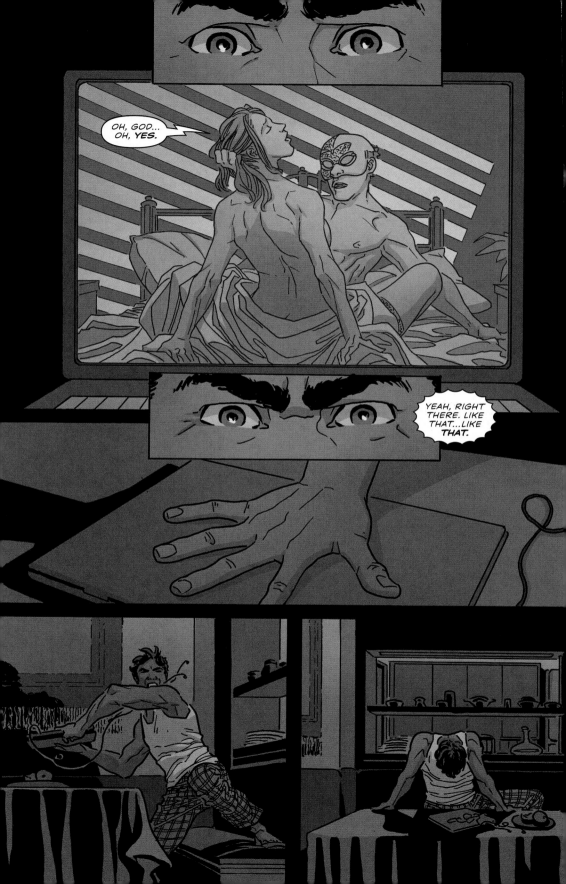

USHWICK,
ROOKLYN
Bushwick Av-
Aberdeen Street
EXIT
KNOCK
KNOCK
IT'S BEEN A WHILE. I NEED TO CALL IN THAT FAVOR...
...SENSEI.

DANI
2020

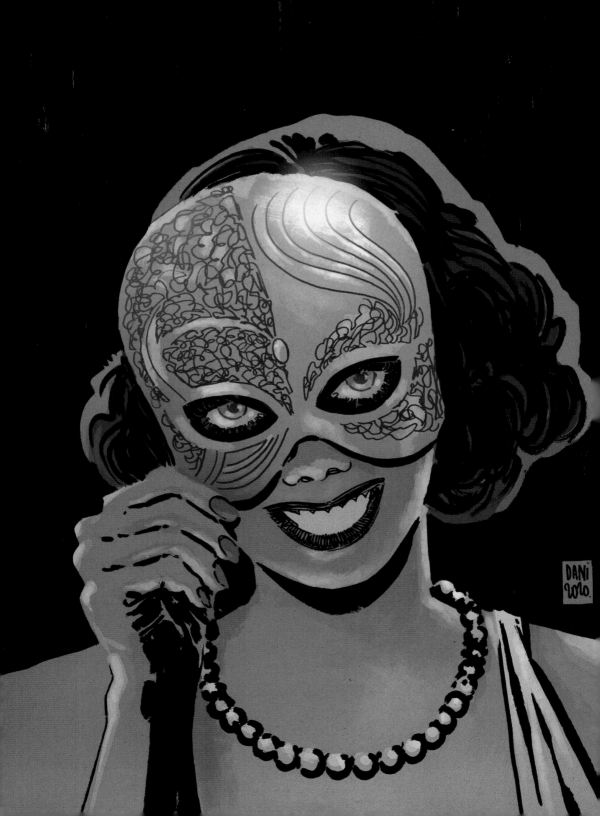

SHWICK, ROOKLYN
'KAY, LET'S CHECK THIS SHIT OUT.
ALL RIGHT, BUT IT'S... IT'S PRETTY GRAPHIC.
DON'T WORRY, HACKERS ARE LIKE DOCTORS--WE'VE SEEN EVERYTHING.
EAH, T THIS S MY VIFE.
MAN, THIS IS ROUGH TO WATCH, AND I DIDN'T PUT A RING ON HER. I FEEL FOR YOU, DUDE.
THANKS.
OH MY GOD...THAT FEELS SO AMAZING.
AND YOU KNOW WHAT THE WORST PART IS?
YOU CAN TELL HOW INTO IT SHE IS. I MEAN IT'S, LIKE, OBVIOUS SHE ISN'T FAKING...NO OFFENSE.
THANKS A LOT.
HOA, SHE'S XIBLE, TOO. I N'T BEEN ABLE O THAT SINCE RIED OUT FOR EER IN NINTH GRADE.
OKAY, THAT'S ENOUGH.
YOU WANT MY HELP, RIGHT?
YEAH, AND SO FAR THIS IS NOT HELPING.

TRUST ME, DUDE, SENSEI KNOWS WHAT SHE'S DOING. THAT'S WHY YOU CAME TO ME, RIGHT?
SO WHAT DO YOU SEE SO FAR--I MEAN TECHNICALLY?
SHIT'S SOPHISTICATED, YO--I MEAN, AS FAR AS SECRET SEX-VIDS GO.
TWO CAMERAS. SWITCHING ANGLES. DUDE KNOWS WHAT HE'S DOING, AND I BET HE'S DONE THIS BEFORE.
THE MASK? HE KNOWS IF HE PIXELATED HIS FACE, SOMEBODY LIKE ME COULD UN-PIXELATE IT.
TRACKING HIM DOWN COULD BE HARD. THESE INTERNET PORN FREAKS ARE CRAZY STEALTH.
BUT I CAN FIGURE OUT IF HE ALREADY UPLOADED THIS SHIT SOME-WHERE.
HOW'RE YOUR KIDS DOIN'?
CONFUSED RIGHT NOW. HONESTLY I DON'T KNOW WHAT'S GONNA HAPPEN NOW EITHER...I MEAN, LIFE GETS STRESSFUL SOMETIMES AND PEOPLE MAKE MISTAKES...
...BUT HO
I SUPPOS
TO FORGIVE
FOR THIS? H
I SUPPOSE
TRUST HER
SEE? THAT'S WHY I DON'T EVEN DATE.
HONESTLY, MY IDEAL SEX PARTNER'S A ROBOT. LIKE THAT A.I. ROBOT CHICK IN EX MACHINA--THE MOVIE, NOT THE COMIC.
FIND ANYTHING YET?
GETTIN' THERE, YO. CHILL. JUST CHILL.

BY THE WAY, IF YOU NNA RETIRE FROM AT-HOME DAD, WE'RE DING AN APP AT THIS RT-UP I'M WORKING E NEED CODERS AND OBODY'S BETTER THAN YOU.
WHAT KIND OF APP?
NASA
DUDES MADE ME SIGN A NONDISCLOSURE, BUT TRUST ME, SHIT'S GONNA BE *LIT.*
LET'S JUST SAY WHEN WE HACK THE NEXT RUSSIAN ELECTION, YOU MIGHT WANT TO THANK SENSEI.
'KAY, I GOT SOMETHING.
YOU WANT THE BAD NEWS... OR THE BAD NEWS?
ESS I'LL THE BAD EWS.
IT'S ALREADY POSTED.
YOU'RE FUCKING KIDDING ME. WHERE?
THAT'S THE *SECOND* BAD NEWS. I DON'T KNOW EXACTLY...
...BUT SOMEWHERE ON THE *DARK WEB.*

THAT'S THE TELL. I JUST, WELL, SCANNED BOUT A MILLION SERVERS TH A PROGRAM I DESIGNED, GOT A MATCH ON A KNOWN K WEB SERVER. IT'S WHERE YOU'LL FIND CHILD PORN, NUFF-VIDS, HATE GROUP CHAT ROOMS. SHIT'S CALLED DARK FOR A REASON.
CAN YOU TELL WHERE THE SERVER IS?
NEED TO DIG MORE FOR THAT. COULD BE BANGLA-DESH, VENEZUELA, PHILIPPINES, OR RUSSIA. THERE'S SOME RUSSIAN LETTERS IN THE CODE, BUT 99 PERCENT OF THAT'S A SMOKESCREEN. PEOPLE LOVE TO BLAME RUSSIANS.
BUT YOU DON'T THINK IT'S UP PUBLICLY RIGHT NOW, RIGHT?
NOT WITH THIS CODE, BUT THAT DOESN'T MEAN HE HASN'T ALTERED IT.
IF YOU CAN FIND IT, HOW COME--
THE COPS CAN'T? LET'S JUST SAY POWERFUL PEOPLE KNOW IT'S ALL THERE. WHICH TELLS YOU ALL YOU NEED TO KNOW, RIGHT?
CAN YOU GET IN?
CAN? YES. WHEN? DUNNO.
IT'S A PUMPED-UP FIREWALL, BUT I'M SURE I CAN FIND A WAY.
BUT LET'S SAY WE FIND HIM, WHAT'S NEXT? I MEAN IF YOU'RE PLANNING TO GO LIAM NEESON ON THIS DUDE, I CAN'T GET IN THE MIDDLE OF THAT SHIT.
JUST FIND OUT WHO HE IS...
...AND EAVE THE REST TO ME.

BZZZ BZZZ
You didn't send the money, Jennifer. Very VERY naughty.
You're going to regret this I'm afraid.
message
WELL, THIS IS QUITE EMBARRASSING.
I'M NOT EXACTLY SURE HOW TO TELL YOU THIS, BUT I...WELL, I MADE A VERY BIG MISTAKE.

AT THAT COCKTAIL PARTY THE OTHER NIGHT WITH ANGELA...I MET SOMEONE, THROUGH HER, ALTHOUGH THEY WERE ONLY ACQUAINTANCES, IT TURNS OUT...
YOU MET HIM, TOO...AT **PER SE**... THE GUY WHO GAVE US THE RECOMMENDATIONS.
I REMEMBER.
I REMEMBER, TOO. WHERE ARE YOU GOING WITH THIS?
THIS MAN AND I... WE HAD AN ENCOUNTER, A **FLING,** WHATEVER YOU WANT TO CALL IT...AND UNFORTUNATELY THINGS HAVE GOTTEN COMPLICATED.
COMPLICATED?
COMPLICATED **HOW?**
HE'S BLACKMAILING ME...OR TRYING TO.
HOW IS HE BLACKMAILING YOU?
HE FILMED US.
I CONTACTED THE POLICE, BUT THERE'S NOT MUCH THEY CAN DO, OR **WANT** TO DO, I'M NOT SURE WHAT THE DIFFERENCE IS.
IT DOESN'T HELP THAT I DON'T KNOW WHO HE IS.
HOW IS THAT POSSIBLE?
I THOUGHT YOU SAID YOU WERE **INTRODUCED** TO HIM.
I WAS. BUT I THINK...I THINK HE WAS USING A FAKE NAME.

THIS IS *BEYOND* DISTURBING, ENNIFER, *PARTICULARLY* BECAUSE IT INVOLVES WHAT WAS SUPPOSED TO BE A PROFESSIONAL EVENT HOSTED BY ONE OF THIS FIRM'S MOST IMPORTANT NEW CLIENTS.
I'M SO SORRY.
I KNOW I MADE A HUGE MISTAKE, BUT HOW DO YOU THINK *I* FEEL?
IT'S NOT LIKE I INTENDED TO MEET THIS GUY...AND OBVIOUSLY I WOULDN'T BE SHARING MY PERSONAL AFFAIRS WITH YOU UNLESS I *HAD* TO.
ALREADY OING OUGH A AT HOME AUSE OF BECAUSE OLD MY BAND AS VELL.
I'M TELLING *YOU* BECAUSE I DON'T WANT YOU TO BE BLINDSIDED IF THIS VIDEO GOES PUBLIC AND IT BECOMES AN ISSUE WITH CLIENTS.
THANK YOU *SO MUCH* FOR YOUR THOUGHTFULNESS AND PROFESSION-ALISM. THAT WHAT YOU WANT TO HEAR?
YOU'VE ALREADY BEEN DISTRACTED AT WORK LATELY, MAYBE IT'S ALL RELATED.
REGARDLESS, AS A PARTNER OF THIS FIRM, YOUR PERSONAL AFFAIRS SHOULD *REMAIN* PERSONAL.
FOR GOD'S SAKE, JENNIFER. YOU KNOW HOW IMPORTANT THIS IS FOR US, AND YET YOU CHOOSE TO USE *THIS* SITUATION TO PICK UP A GUY?
I DIDN'T PICK HIM UP.
THEN WHAT DO YOU CALL IT?
DON'T LIKE IR TONE RIGHT W, JAMES, NOR I THINK IT'S PPROPRIATE.
APPROPRIATE? IS THAT SERIOUSLY THE WORD *YOU* JUST USED?
I THINK JAMES AND I NEED TO DISCUSS ALL OF THIS IN PRIVATE... WE'LL BE IN TOUCH.
FINE.

HELLO.
HI, THANK YOU FOR LETTING ME--
MOMMY!
I MISSED YOU SO MUCH.
OH, I MISSED YOU TOO, SWEETIE.
WHEN CAN WE GO HOME ALREADY?
I'M NOT SURE. DADDY AND I NEED TO DISCUSS SOME THINGS.
WHY? I WANT TO SLEEP IN MY ROOM.
I KNOW. SO DO I.
WHY'RE *YOU* HERE?
HEY, I...I DIDN'T KNOW YOU WERE GOING TO BE HERE.
YOU CAN'T JUST COME BY AND--
I TOLD HER SHE COULD COME SEE THE KIDS.
CAN WE TALK FOR A SEC?
...IN THE OTHER ROOM.

IT'S COOL, THE KIDS WANTED TO SEE YOU. SORRY I SNAPPED LIKE THAT.
YOU HAVE NOTHING TO BE SORRY FOR.
SO...HOW *ARE* YOU?
DOES IT MATTER?
IT MATTERS TO ME.
DOES IT?
LOOK, I DESERVE ALL OF THIS, I *KNOW* THAT. IF I COULD UNDO WHAT I DID, I WOULD.
WHY WOULD YOU MAKE A DIFFERENT DECISION? BECAUSE YOU GOT CAUGHT AND YOU KNOW THE CONSEQUENCES? LIKE YOU COULDN'T *ANTICIPATE* ANY OF THIS?
I DIDN'T INTEND FOR YOU TO GET HURT.
BULLSHIT.
YOU WERE THINKING ABOUT ONE PERSON--*YOURSELF.* YOU DIDN'T GIVE A FUCK ABOUT HURTING ME OR YOUR FUCKING FAMILY WHEN YOU WENT INTO THAT HOTEL ROOM WITH THAT *MASKED FREAK.*
THAT'S NOT HOW IT WAS.
I KNOW HOW IT LOOKS, BUT THAT'S NOT HOW I *FELT.* I DIDN'T KNOW ABOUT THE MASK WHEN I...
IT WAS JUST ALL HAPPENING... SO FAST--
BUT IT WAS STILL *"SO AMAZING,"* RIGHT?
I GOT LOST IN THE MOMENT... SUCKED IN...I--
KNOCK KNOCK

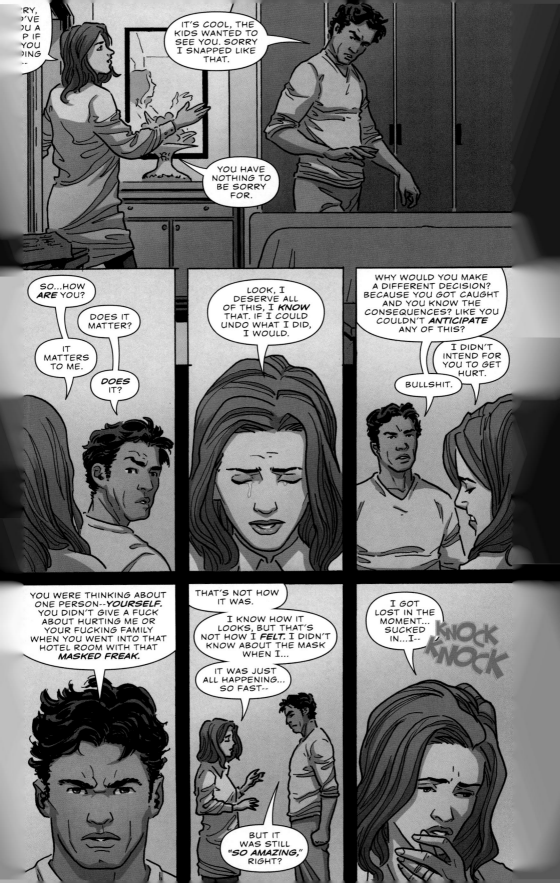

HEY, CAN YOU BOTH KEEP IT DOWN? THE KIDS ARE RIGHT IN THE OTHER ROOM AND WE CAN HEAR EVERY WORD YOU SAY.
FUCK. SORRY, DAD.
HE'S RIGHT, WE CAN'T DO THIS. IT'S JUST MAKING THINGS WORSE.
I KNOW YOU MIGHT NEVER FORGIVE ME, BUT I OBVIOUSLY HAD NO IDEA THAT HE WAS FILMING US, OR WOULD TRY TO BLACKMAIL ME.
PLEASE...SPARE ME THE VICTIM ROUTINE, ALL RIGHT? THIS ISN'T A ME TOO. CALL IT WHAT IT WAS-- CHEATING.
OKAY. I GUESS I SHOULD GO.
BY THE WAY, I TOLD PARTNERS WHAT HAPPE AND I COULD LOSE PARTNERSHIP AT THE I'VE ALREADY LOST FAMILY, BUT I GUESS YO RIGHT--I'M NOT ACTUA A VICTIM.
WAIT.
WHAT IF I CAN FIND THIS GUY, ALEX MILES, OR WHATEVER THE HELL HIS NAME IS?
WHAT IF WE CAN BRING THE EVIDENCE TO THE COPS? WOULD THAT SAVE YOUR JOB?
MAYBE. BUT HOW COULD YOU FIND HIM?
MAYBE I ALREADY DID.

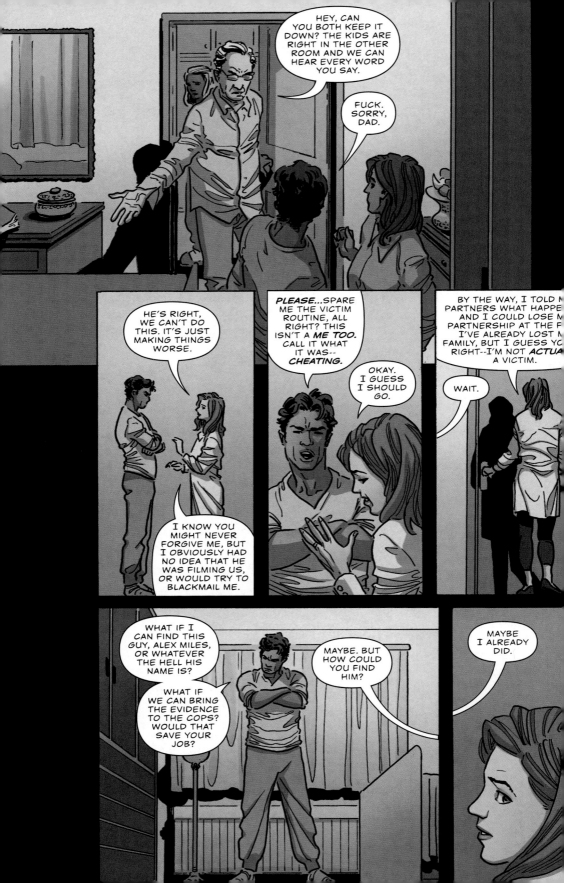

LOOK, I GOTTA BE HONEST...
...I DON'T KNOW IF I CAN GET PAST THIS. I MEAN, NOW THAT THOSE IMAGES ARE IN MY HEAD, THEY'RE THERE FOREVER.
I'M SO, SO SORRY, MATT.
SORRIES WON'T HELP EITHER.
THEN WHY ARE YOU DOING THIS?
WHY NOT JUST FORGET ABOUT ME? MOVE ON.
I CAN'T DO THAT.
NO MATTER WHAT HAPPENS WITH US, YOU'RE MY KIDS' MOTHER. IF WE CAN STOP THAT VIDEO FROM EVER GOING PUBLIC, I'LL DO WHATEVER IT TAKES.
WHATEVER YOUR REASONS, I APPRECIATE ALL OF THIS.
SO WHO'S THIS FRIEND OF YOURS?
SOMEBODY I USED TO WORK WITH BACK IN THE DAY. A PROGRAMMER-SLASH-HACKER.
OH GOD, THEY SAW THE VIDEO, TOO?
THIS IS SO MORTIFYING.
TELL ME ABOUT IT.

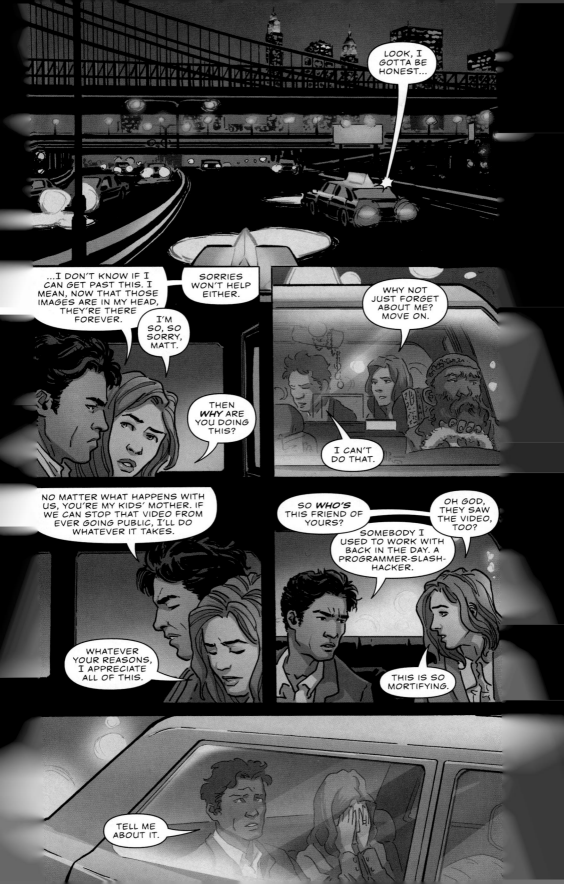

SORRY, I'M NOT A WINE CHICK, BUT HERE IN BUSHWICK WE GOT THE BEST IPAs IN THE WORLD. WELL, MAYBE NOT THE BEST BUT...
I'M GOOD.
I'LL HAVE ONE.
YOU'VE BEEN UNDER A LOT OF STRESS, I'M SURE. THIS SHIT'S CRAZY. THESE DAYS, THERE'RE CAMERAS EVERYWHERE. IT'S LIKE WE'RE ALL IN A REALITY TV SHOW THAT NEVER ENDS.
BUT I GOTTA SAY, YOU HAVE A DOPE BODY. HOW MANY TIMES A WEEK YOU HIT THE GYM?
LATELY? I HAVEN'T HAD A CHANCE TO GO AT ALL.
NO GYM AND YOU GOT ***THAT BODY?*** DANG.
THANK YOU.
I DON'T LIKE TO GET IN THE MIDDLE OF OTHER PEOPLE'S BUSINESS, BUT I HOPE YOU GUYS STAY TOGETHER. I SENSE A VIBE HERE, A ***POSITIVE*** VIBE. AND YOU'VE GOT KIDS TOGETHER, DON'T FORGET THAT.
CAN I MAKE A LITTLE SUGGESTION?
SURE.
NEXT TIME YOU WANNA STEP OUT, WHY NOT A ***THREESOME?***
NOT WITH ME--I GOT ENOUGH DRAMA, BUT I KNOW PEOPLE WHO SAY THREESOMES SAVED THEIR MARRIAGE.
LOOK, I APPRECIATE THE FREE MARRIAGE COUNSELING, BUT CAN YOU JUST SHOW HER WHAT WE FOUND OUT?
IT'S COOL, I'M DONE PREACHING. BUT IT WOULD SUCK IF YOU THREW YOUR MARRIAGE AWAY, IS ALL I'M SAYIN'.

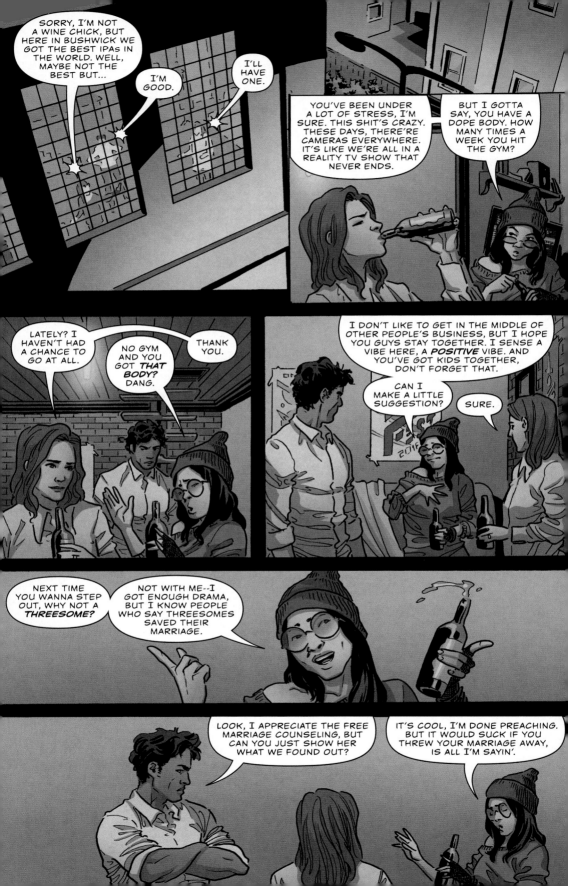

AT AM
OOKING
AT?
THE SITE WHERE YOUR SEX VID WAS UPLOADED.
THAT'S
T ME.
YEAH, BUT THAT'S HIM.
HOW CAN YOU TELL?
WELL, HATE TO GET GRAPHIC, BUT...
MY DUDE'S GOT A CURVED DICK, LIKE THE LETTER C. SORRY, BUT THAT SHIT'S HARD TO MISS.
T, SO I
RIGHT, I
N'T THE
RST?
NO, BUT YOU MIGHT'VE BEEN THE HUNDRED AND FIRST. THERE ARE DOZENS OF VIDS JUST LIKE THIS ONE. LOOKS LIKE THEY'RE ALL SHOT IN HOTEL ROOMS.
FUCKING CREEP. IS THIS SITE PUBLIC? CAN ANYBODY SEE THESE?
THIS SITE LOOKS PRIVATE, NOT A LOT OF VIEWS. MAYBE HE'S GOT FRIENDS WATCHING OR WHATEVER, BUT THAT DOESN'T MEAN IT'S NOT SOME-WHERE ELSE, TOO.
HOW CAN WE STOP HIM?
THAT'S WHERE MATT COMES IN.
AS YOU SEE, ALEX MILES, OR WHATEVER THE FUCK HIS NAME IS, HAS A MASK ON IN ALL THE VIDEOS, BUT THE WOMEN DON'T.
YEAH, SO?
SO I CAPTURED IMAGES OF ALL OF THE WOMEN, THEN USED FACIAL RECOGNITION SOFTWARE TO CROSS-MATCH THEM.
I HAVEN'T GOTTEN THROUGH ALL THE IMAGES YET. ON SOME I COULDN'T GET A CLEAR ENOUGH SHOT, AND SOME I COULDN'T FIND MATCHES.
BUT I DID GET SOME NAMES.

THIS IS LARA FISCHER. DID A LITTLE MORE RESEARCH ON HER. SHE USED TO RUN A HEDGE FUND, BUT LEFT HER COMPANY A YEAR AND A HALF AGO AND APPARENTLY HASN'T WORKED SINCE.
THIS IS SONDRA MCNEIL. ALSO IN MANHATTAN. TRACKED HER FROM A PHOTO AT A GALLERY OPENING IN SOHO SHE ATTENDED LAST SPRING, THEN FOUND HER ON FACEBOOK. WAS A SURGEON AT MOUNT SINAI HOSPITAL-- ALSO NOT CURRENTLY EMPLOYED.
THIS IS BROOKE DAVIDSON. LIVES IN SCARSDALE, BUT I CAN'T FIND ANY RECENT EMPLOYMENT HISTORY FOR HER EITHER.
WOW...
...YOU GUYS ARE AMAZING. SO THEY'RE ALL IN THE NYC AREA?
MOST, BUT SOME ARE IN LA, CHICAGO, MIAMI, PARIS, BERLIN... AND ONE IN TOKYO. THIS GUY GETS AROUND.
AND I'LL TELL YOU SOMETHIN' ELSE ABOUT MY DUDE...
...HE DOESN'T SEEM TO HAVE A TYPE. DIFFERENT RACES, DIFFERENT SIZES. HE'S ALL OVER THE FREAKIN' MAP.
I'M NOT SURE ABOUT THAT. THEY ALL WERE SUCCESFUL AND MANY HAD HIGH-LEVEL EXECUTIVE POSITIONS THAT MOST OF THEM DON'T HAVE NOW.
SO THAT'S HOW THE SICK BASTARD GETS OFF...
DESTROYING WOMEN'S LIVES A WAY HE POSSIB CAN.

AN STOP HIM, CAN GET THE R VICTIMS TO IE FORWARD AND--
ADMIT WHAT?
SO NOW YOU ADMIT IT?
THAT I'M A VICTIM.
SHE'S GOT A POINT THERE, MATT. I HEARD YOU SAY THE WORD.
THE IMPORTANT THING NOW IS THAT WE DON'T HAVE TIME TO WASTE. WE HAVE TO MOVE QUICKLY--BEFORE HE DECIDES TO PUT THESE ON PORNHUB, OR SEND THEM TO YOUR CLIENTS.
WHAT CAN I DO?
HELP ME FIND THE WOMEN. MAYBE ONE OF THEM CAN TELL US HOW TO FIND THIS GUY.
I HAVE ANOTHER IDEA. HE'S IN A MASK IN THE VIDEOS, BUT HE WASN'T IN A MASK AT THAT BAR IN HUDSON YARDS, OR THE HOTEL BAR WHERE I MET HIM, OR WHEN HE CAME TO MY OFFICE TO SEE ME, OR AT PER SE, OR AT THAT ROCK CONCERT.
THAT IS A GOOD IDEA.
CAN WE GET THE SECURITY VIDEO SOMEHOW?
DID YOU FORGET WHO YOU'RE TALKING TO?
BABY, I'M LIKE A SUPERHERO WITHOUT THE TIGHT ASS OR THE SPANDEX. I CAN DO ANYTHING.

BRRRNNGGG BRRRRINNGG
DETECTIVE RAMIREZ.
HI, DETECTIVE. IT'S JENNIFER... JENNIFER RYAN.
WHO?
I SPOKE TO YOU IN YOUR OFFICE YESTERDAY.
OH, RIGHT, THE WOMAN WHOSE DATE MADE THE SEX TAPE.
HE WASN'T MY DATE, AND I DON'T APPRECIATE YOUR BELITTLING TONE.
SORRY, SORRY, WHAT CAN I DO FOR YOU, MS. RYAN?
I THINK I...WELL. MY TEAM HAS MADE A BREAK-THROUGH.
YOUR TEAM
ARE DOZENS OF DETECTIVE. IF I OTHER WOMEN FORWARD, WE'LL STRONG CASE ST THIS GUY.
WHAT'S THE GUY'S NAME?
I DON'T KNOW IT YET, BUT I WILL KNOW IT. SOON.
GREAT. WELL, THE I'M LOOKING FORW TO ALL OF THIS INFORMATION.

LARA...I'M JENNIFER RYAN, THE WOMAN WHO CONTACTED YOU ABOUT FINDING THE MAN WHO--
NOT INTERESTED.
WE'RE NOT ALONE, LARA. IF YOU'D JUST TALK TO ME FOR A FEW MINUTES, WE CAN FIND HIM, MAKE HIM PAY FOR WHAT HE'S DONE, AND PROBABLY STILL DOING.
YOU KNOW WHO THIS MAN IS, DON'T YOU?
PLEASE. I'VE BEEN THROUGH ENOUGH. I...I CAN'T HANDLE THIS. NOT NOW.
ARIA, I WAS NDERING IF I LD JUST MEET ITH YOU, TO SCUSS HOW WE CAN--
FUCK OFF.
...IF YOU'D JUST GIVE ME A MINUTE TO EXPLAIN, I COULD...HELLO? HELLO?
NO WAY.
I UNDERSTAND, SONDRA, BUT--
CLICK
BZZZZBZZZZ
YES, BROOKE, THANK YOU FOR GETTING BACK TO...
YES, YES, I'D LOVE TO MEET YOU...TODAY? YES, THAT TOTALLY WORKS.

BROOKE?
JENNIFER?
YES. THANK YOU FOR MEETING ME.
NO, THANK YOU. PLEASE, SIT DOWN.
IT'S IMPORTANT TO KNOW THAT WE'RE NOT THE ONLY VICTIMS. THERE ARE DOZENS OF OTHER WOMEN OUT THERE, AND WHEN WE COME FORWARD, THEY'LL JOIN US, I'M SURE OF IT.
I CAN'T TELL YOU HOW MUCH I APPRECIATE WHAT YOU'RE DOING, AND I'LL DO ANYTHING I CAN TO HELP.
I'VE BEEN HARBORING SO MUCH RAGE AGAINST THAT MAN FOR SO LONG. WHAT HE DID TO ME-- MAKING ME FEEL LIKE WE HAD A ***SPECIAL CONNECTION*** SO I'D LET MY DEFENSES DOWN, THEN BLACKMAILING ME.
AND AFTERWARDS-- ALL THOSE NIGHTMARES, THE SELF-MEDICATING, AND I FELT SO ***ALONE.*** I HAD NO IDEA THERE WERE SO MANY OTHERS LIKE ME... LIKE ***US.***
I CAN'T WAIT TO FACE HIM IN COURT, WHERE HE CAN'T HIDE BEHIND THAT HORRIBLE MASK ANY LONGER, WHEN HE HAS TO FACE US, ***ALL*** OF HIS VICTIMS.
THAT WILL BE A BEAUTIFUL DAY.

GREAT NEWS. ONE OF THE WOMEN JUST SAID YES.
WESOME.
SHE'S REALLY ANGRY AND FIRED UP--SHE'LL BE GREAT. AND WITH HER ON BOARD MORE WOMEN WILL COME FORWARD, I'M SURE.
THE ONLY PROBLEM IS I STILL DON'T KNOW HIS REAL NAME. HE TOLD HER HIS NAME WAS STEVEN, SO HE'S PROBABLY USED ALIASES WITH ALL HIS VICTIMS.
I HAVE SOME NEWS ON THAT FRONT.
SENSEI HACKED INTO YOUR OFFICE'S SECURITY COMPANY, AND SECURITY AT THE HUDSON YARDS RESTAURANT, BUT IT LOOKS LIKE SOMEBODY BEAT HER TO IT.
FUCK.
BUT I THINK WE HIT PAYDIRT ON ANOTHER LEAD. I JUST NEED YOU TO HELP ME ID HIM.
THAT'S AMAZING. 'M ON MY WAY BACK IGHT NOW, MAYBE I CAN MEET YOU AT YOUR PARENTS' LATER?
COOL.
HEY, MATT...
...I'M SERIOUS ABOUT GOING TO COUNSELING IF YOU'RE UP FOR IT.
WE'LL SEE.
I'LL TAKE A WE'LL SEE.

SCARSDALE
I LOVE WHEN THEY START GETTING SOME HOPE, DON'T YOU?
IT IS A GREAT RUSH, ISN'T IT?
THE BEST.
LAWYERS, ALWAYS SO SMUG...
...AND THINK THEY HAVE ALL THE ANSWERS.
SHE'S OUR FIFTH LAWYER, ISN'T SHE? OR IS SHE THE SIXTH?
SIXTH, I BELIEVE.
SIX LAWYERS! AND SHE HAS ABSOLUTELY NO IDEA I'M YOUR WIFE. SHE THINKS SHE'S A STEP AHEAD, BUT SHE'S REALLY AT LEAST THREE BEHIND.
AND NOW COMES THE BEST PART. WHEN WE TOTALLY DESTROY HER.
ARE YOU SURE, DARLING? MAYBE IT'S TIME TO MOVE ON FROM THIS ONE.
WHY ON EARTH WOULD WE DO THAT?
JUST A GUT FEELING. MAYBE IT WAS A MISTAKE TO MEET HER. TOO RECKLESS.
COME ON, WE'RE JUST HAVING A LITTLE FUN. ISN'T THAT WHAT IT'S ALL ABOUT?

AND HE'S JUST FFING. THAT'S AT LAWYERS LWAYS DO. HEY BLUFF.
YOU'RE RIGHT, I'M PROBABLY JUST BEING PARANOID.
THIS IS THE BEST PART.
PUT IT ON.
OH MY GOD...THAT FEELS SO AMAZING.
YES, JENNIFER... OH YES IT DOES.

DANI
2021 V.

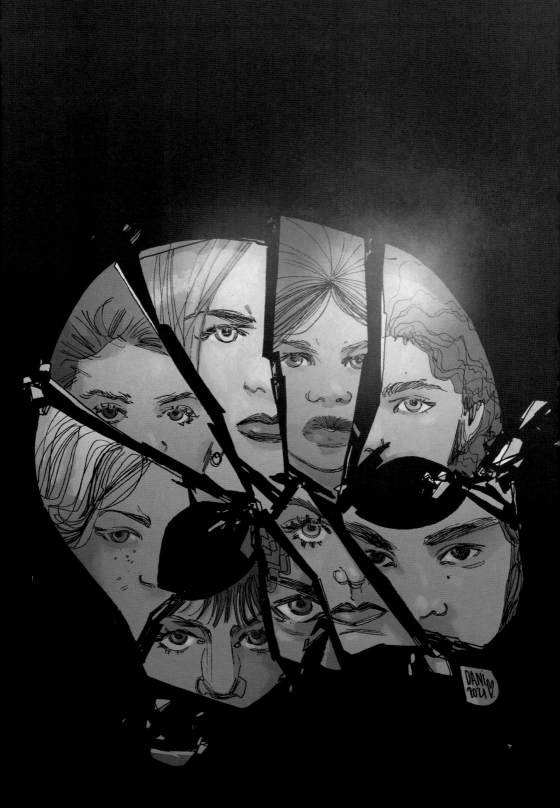

NO, DON'T!
YOU CAN'T DO THAT, DO YOU UNDERSTAND ME? THAT'S *EXTREMELY* DANGEROUS.
DIDN'T I TELL YOU TO WATCH YOUR BROTHER?
SORRY.
SHUT OFF THE TV RIGHT NOW AND GET YOUR SHOES ON.
WHY DO WE HAVE TO GO THERE *AGAIN?*
BECAUSE THAT'S THE SITUATION RIGHT NOW.
BUT ALL MY TOYS ARE HERE AND GRANDPA SNORES SO LOUD I CAN HEAR IT THROUGH THE WALLS.
LISTEN TO YOUR MOTHER.
COME ON, GET READY TO GO. WE'RE LATE.
BUT I DON'T WAN--
I SAID, LET'S GO.
WE LOVE YOU, SWEETIE.

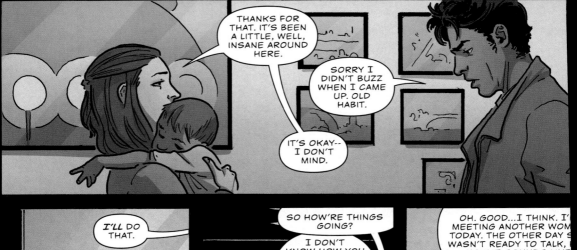

THANKS FOR THAT. IT'S BEEN A LITTLE, WELL, INSANE AROUND HERE.

SORRY I DIDN'T BUZZ WHEN I CAME UP. OLD HABIT.

IT'S OKAY-- I DON'T MIND.

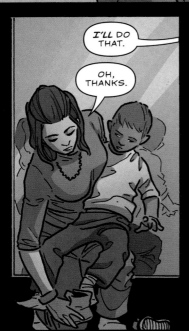

I'LL DO THAT.

OH, THANKS.

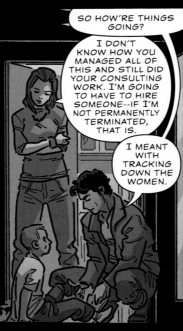

SO HOW'RE THINGS GOING?

I DON'T KNOW HOW YOU MANAGED ALL OF THIS AND STILL DID YOUR CONSULTING WORK. I'M GOING TO HAVE TO HIRE SOMEONE--IF I'M NOT PERMANENTLY TERMINATED, THAT IS.

I MEANT WITH TRACKING DOWN THE WOMEN.

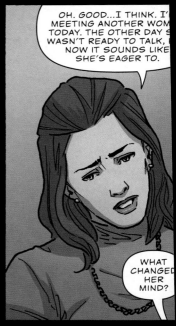

OH. GOOD...I THINK. I' MEETING ANOTHER WOM TODAY. THE OTHER DAY S WASN'T READY TO TALK, NOW IT SOUNDS LIKE SHE'S EAGER TO.

WHAT CHANGED HER MIND?

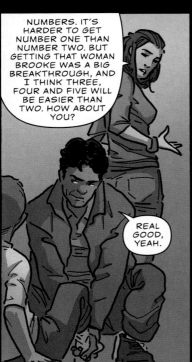

NUMBERS. IT'S HARDER TO GET NUMBER ONE THAN NUMBER TWO. BUT GETTING THAT WOMAN BROOKE WAS A BIG BREAKTHROUGH, AND I THINK THREE, FOUR AND FIVE WILL BE EASIER THAN TWO. HOW ABOUT YOU?

REAL GOOD, YEAH.

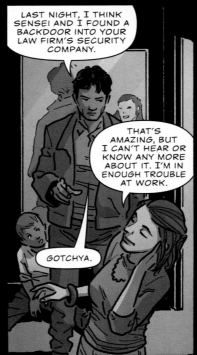

LAST NIGHT, I THINK SENSEI AND I FOUND A BACKDOOR INTO YOUR LAW FIRM'S SECURITY COMPANY.

THAT'S AMAZING, BUT I CAN'T HEAR OR KNOW ANY MORE ABOUT IT. I'M IN ENOUGH TROUBLE AT WORK.

GOTCHYA.

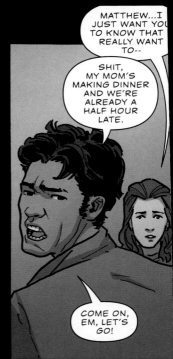

MATTHEW...I JUST WANT YOU TO KNOW THAT I REALLY WANT TO--

SHIT, MY MOM'S MAKING DINNER AND WE'RE ALREADY A HALF HOUR LATE.

COME ON, EM, LET'S GO!

IT WAS A FEW YEARS AGO. I JUST GOT OUT OF A RELATIONSHIP AND WANTED TO MEET NEW PEOPLE SO I WENT ONLINE.

"HE SAID HE WAS IN TOWN FROM L.A. AND WAS LOOKING FOR SOMETHING *CASUAL.* ACTUALLY, THIS WAS FINE WITH ME BECAUSE I WAS REBOUNDING MYSELF AT THE TIME.

"LUCKY ME, THE FIRST GUY I SWIPED ON WAS *SEBASTIAN PORTER.*

"IT SEEMED LIKE WE HAD THIS AMAZING CONNECTION. WE TALKED ABOUT MOVIES, TRAVEL, OUR FAVORITE BOOKS, AND THE CONVERSATION SEEMED SO *EFFORTLESS.*

"LATER, I REALIZED *WHY* WE HAD SO MUCH IN COMMON..."

...HE'D BEEN STALKING ME ONLINE. I LINKED MY INSTAGRAM TO MY BUMBLE PROFILE, SO IT WASN'T EXACTLY HARD FOR HIM TO DO HIS RESEARCH.

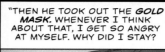

I HAVE TO HAND IT TO HIM, HE WAS GOOD. OUR CONNECTION FELT LEGIT.

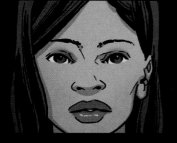

"HE SAID IT WAS HIS LAST NIGHT IN NEW YORK AND HE HAD A FLIGHT BACK TO L.A. IN THE MORNING, SO WE WENT TO HIS HOTEL ROOM.

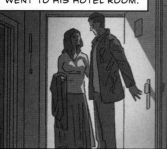

"UP UNTIL THAT POINT, EVERYTHING SEEMED NORMAL. I THOUGHT HE WAS A GREAT GUY AND I WAS ACTUALLY DIS-APPOINTED HE WAS LEAVING TOWN. HOW FUCKED UP IS *THAT?*

"THEN HE TOOK OUT THE *GOLD MASK.* WHENEVER I THINK ABOUT THAT, I GET SO ANGRY AT MYSELF. WHY DID I STAY?

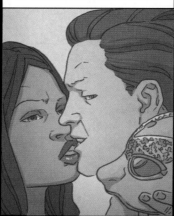

"IT WAS SO FUCKING WEIRD. WHY DIDN'T I JUST *RUN?*"

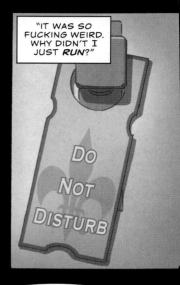

DO NOT DISTURB

I THINK IT'S BECAUSE I FORGET HOW HE MADE ME *FEEL* THAT NIGHT. HE CLAIMED HE WAS A C.F.O., LIKE ME, SO WE HAD THE FINANCIAL CONNECTION, BUT THERE WAS MORE TO IT THAN THAT. I WAS GOING THROUGH A BREAKUP, I WAS VULNERABLE, AND HE MADE ME FEEL SPECIAL, LIKE HE TRULY CARED.

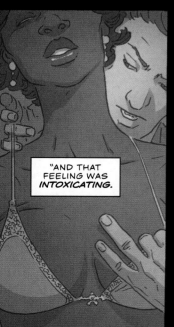

"AND THAT FEELING WAS *INTOXICATING.*

"I HAVE TO ADMIT, THE SEX WAS GREAT. HE DEFINITELY KNEW WHAT HE WAS DOING IN THAT DEPARTMENT.

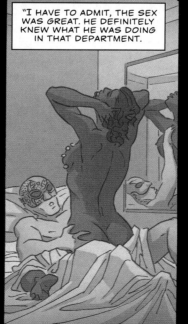

"WHEN I LEFT IN THE MORNING, I HAD NO REGRETS. *NONE.*

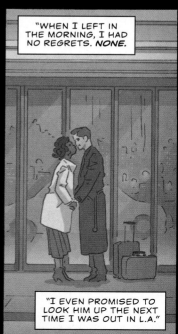

"I EVEN PROMISED TO LOOK HIM UP THE NEXT TIME I WAS OUT IN L.A."

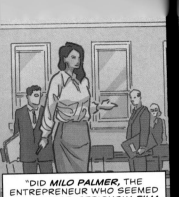

"IT SEEMED IMPOSSIBLE, SURREAL. WHY WOULD HE *DO* THAT?

"DID *MILO PALMER*, THE ENTREPRENEUR WHO SEEMED SO SINCERE, SERIOUSLY *FILM US* HAVING SEX?

"WATCHING THE VIDEO WAS EVEN MORE SURREAL. IT WAS LIKE I WASN'T WATCHING MYSELF. WATCHING IT, I WAS THINKING, THAT *CAN'T* BE *ME*-- THAT HAS TO BE SOMEONE ELSE. I'VE NEVER FELT SO DETACHED FROM REALITY.

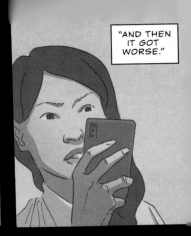

"AND THEN IT GOT WORSE."

HE WANTED TWENTY-FIVE THOUSAND DOLLARS *IN BITCOIN*, OR HE'D PUT THE VIDEO ONLINE AND SEND IT TO MY EDITORS AND COWORKERS. AS HEAD OF A PUBLISHING COMPANY, I OBVIOUSLY COULDN'T LET THAT HAPPEN.

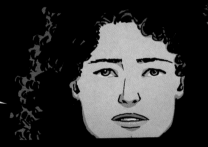

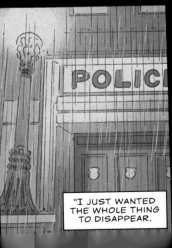

"I HAD NO IDEA WHAT TO DO. I ALMOST WENT TO THE POLICE, BUT I DIDN'T EVEN WANT TO TELL MY FRIENDS BECAUSE I FELT SO EMBARRASSED AND STUPID.

"I JUST WANTED THE WHOLE THING TO DISAPPEAR.

"SO I SENT THE *BITCOIN*, JUST LIKE HE INSTRUCTED ME TO. I HOPED THAT WOULD BE THE END OF IT..."

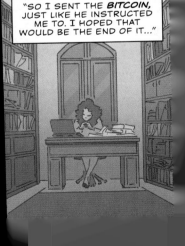

COME, BROOKE DARLING. THERE ARE *SO MANY* OPTIONS FOR OUR NEXT ADVENTURE.
CRYSTAL: AN ANESTHESIOLOGIST AT COLUMBIA PRESBYTERIAN HOSPITAL. HIGHLY REGARDED IN HER FIELD WITH A GREAT FUTURE AHEAD OF HER. IT WOULD BE A SHAME IF SHE LOST IT ALL.
MERCEDES: RUNS ONE OF THE LARGEST P.R. FIRMS IN THE COUNTRY, AND I'M SURE COULDN'T EVEN *IMAGINE* LOSING EVERYTHING, AND HAVING TO START ALL OVER AGAIN.
AH, AND HERE'S AN ENTICING OPTION. JUST TWENTY-TWO, FRESH OUT OF WELLESLEY. YOU REMEMBER? WE MET AT THAT GALLERY OPENING AT SOTHEBY'S LAST MONTH.
OH, THAT RIGHT. O COURSE, T ASPIRING DEALER. S WAS WITH PARENTS WASN'T SHE?
EXACTLY. HER FAMILY WERE MAJOR BENEFACTORS OF THE ARTIST. EXTREMELY WEALTHY FAMILY. MOTHER AND FATHER BOTH HEDGE FUND MANAGERS.
THEY LIVE ON PARK AVENUE AND MALIBU WHEN THEY'RE NOT SAILING AROUND THE WORLD ON THEIR MASSIVE YACHT.
SHE *IS* BEAUTIFUL, ISN'T SHE?
SHE'LL BE A CHALLENGE, BUT YOU KNOW HOW MUCH I LOVE A GOOD CHALLENGE.
IT'S JUST A MATTER OF FINDING HER CRACK AND EXPLOITING IT. SHE SEEMS SO TOGETHER AND SURE OF HERSELF, BUT IT'S JUST A FAÇADE, OF COURSE. THEY *ALL* HAVE A CRACK.

I GOTTA HAND IT TO YOU...
YOUR WIFE IS OT, MAN. SERIOUS. NOW MY PORN AND MY PROFESSIONAL PINION IS THIS SHIT OLDS UP. SHE COUD HAVE A CAREER IN THE BIZ IF SHE WANTED TO--
NOT SAYING SHE SHOULD, JUST SAYING SHE COULD.
GEE, YOU THINK?
I THOUGHT YOU'RE LOOKING FOR CLUES.
I'M MULTI-TASKING, DUDE.
MAYBE IT'S NONE OF MY BUSINESS, BUT WHAT WENT WRONG WITH YOU TWO?
YOU'RE RIGHT. IT IS NONE OF YOUR BUSINESS.
COME ON, I WON'T JUDGE.
FUCK, I'M SO CLOSE TO GETTING IN. I GOTTA GET THAT SECURITY FOOTAGE.
NEED MY HELP?
NAH, I GOT THIS.
COME ON, TELL ME, WHAT HAPPENED WITH YOU TWO? WHY'D SHE STEP OUT?
I DON'T KNOW. ASK HER.
NASA
YOU KNOW WHAT THEY SAY-- THE GUY ALWAYS KNOWS.

OKAY, MAYBE I GOT TOO INVOLVED WITH THE KIDS' SCHEDULES, LOST MY MOJO.
IT'S HARD, KEEPING THINGS FRESH. WE'VE BEEN TOGETHER ALMOST TEN YEARS.
I FEEL LIKE I SHOULD GET A MEDAL OR SOMETHING.
I LOOK AT MY PARENTS, FORTY-SIX YEARS TOGETHER, AND, SERIOUSLY, I DON'T KNOW HOW THEY DO IT.
I SHOULDN'T TALK. MY LONGEST RELATIONSHIP LASTED TWO WEEKENDS--WELL, ALMOST TWO WEEKENDS. BUT I DO KNOW ONE THING: YOU GOTTA KEEP YOUR GAME UP IF YOU WANT TO KEEP YOUR WOMAN.
MAYBE. BUT IT STILL DOESN'T EXCUSE WHAT SHE DID.
IT DOESN'T EXCUSE IT...
BUT IT DOES EXPLAIN IT.
OH SHIT, YOU GOTTA CHECK THIS OUT.
IF IT'S A NEW ANGLE OF JENNIFER AND THAT MASKED GUY WITH THE CURVY DICK, I CAN'T TAKE ANY MORE.
IT'S NOT YOUR WIFE DUDE. COM SEE THIS.
HO'S HE WITH?
THAT'S BROOKE ASTON, THE WOMAN YOUR WIFE WENT TO TALK TO YESTERDAY. AND YOU OTICE ANYTHING UNUSUAL ABOUT THE OTHER WOMAN? THE ONE ON THE BED?
IS SHE...?
YEAH...SHE'S UNCONSCIOUS, MAN.
"I KNOW

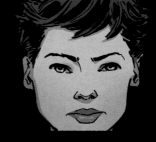

...AND EVERYTHING THAT HAPPENED **BEFORE** I BLACKED OUT.

EVERYTHING.

"I WAS AT **LE BAIN** IN THE MEATPACKING DISTRICT, I CAME WITH A FRIEND, BUT SHE WAS TALKING TO SOME GUY. I WAS PLANNING TO JUST FINISH MY DRINK AND GO HOME...

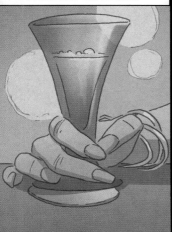

"...BUT THEN **SHE** CAME OVER.

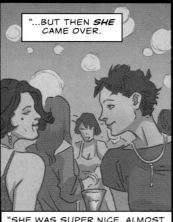

"SHE WAS SUPER NICE, ALMOST **TOO NICE.** SHE WENT ON ABOUT HOW PRETTY I WAS, AND HOW I SHOULD BE A MODEL, AND HOW SHE COULD INTRODUCE ME TO ONE OF THE BIGGEST MODELING AGENTS, WHO HAPPENED TO BE AT THE CLUB.

"HE WAS REALLY SMOOTH, TELLING ME EVERYTHING HE COULD DO FOR MY CAREER AND WHAT A GREAT FUTURE I HAD.

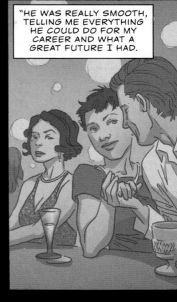

"I WAS GETTING A SUPER SLEAZY VIBE AND TOLD HIM I'M NOT INTERESTED.

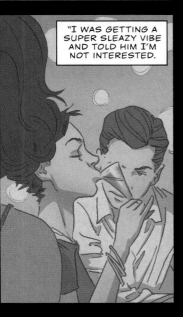

"NEXT THING I KNOW, I'M WAKING UP...

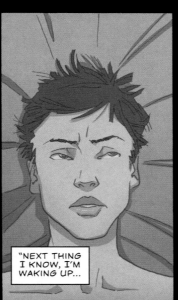

"...AND THEY'RE BOTH STANDING OVER ME."

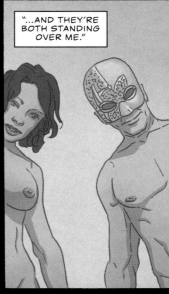

THAT WOMAN'S AS GUILTY AS HE IS, AND I'LL NEVER FORGET THE PERFUME SHE WAS WEARING THAT NIGHT.

EVERY TIME I SMELL IT ON SOMEBODY I WANT TO THROW UP.

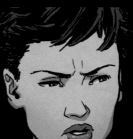

ALMOST READY TO GO? WE NEED TO BE AT THE PIERRE BY SEVEN, THE LATEST.
MY GOD, YOU LOOK **STUNNING.**
THANK YOU.
LMOST MAKES VANT TO FILM A EO WITH ***JUST*** TONIGHT, AND E YOU ALL TO MYSELF.
IS THAT WHAT YOU ***REALLY*** WANT?
YES, BUT I WANT ***YOU*** TO BE HAPPY AS WELL, OF COURSE.
AH, BUT BEFORE WE BEGIN THE NEXT CHAPTER, LET'S END THE LAST, SHALL WE?
VOILA! HER PARTNERS, CO-WORKERS, AND CLIENTS NOV HAVE THE VIDEO. HER LIFE I OFFICIALLY RUINED, WHICH MEANS, OF COURSE, SHE'L NEVER FORGET ABOUT HER EXPERIENCE WITH ME, OR US.
THIS IS WHAT IMMORTALITY EELS LIKE, DARLING. SOAK IT IN, ***EXPERIENCE*** IT.

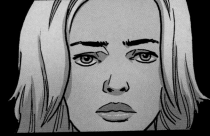

I CAN'T BELIEVE I'M TALKING ABOUT THIS SHIT. I NEVER THOUGHT HE'D COME INTO MY LIFE AGAIN, I THOUGHT I WAS DONE WITH ALL THAT, BUT HERE WE ARE.

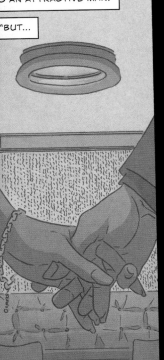

EFINITELY WENT UP TO AT HOTEL ROOM WITH BY CHOICE. WHY NOT? A SINGLE WOMAN AND S AN ATTRACTIVE MAN.

"BUT...

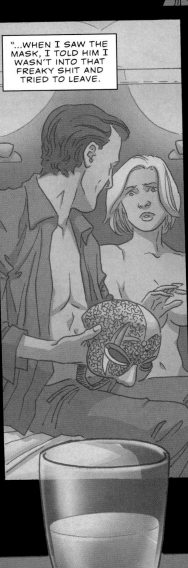

"...WHEN I SAW THE MASK, I TOLD HIM I WASN'T INTO THAT FREAKY SHIT AND TRIED TO LEAVE.

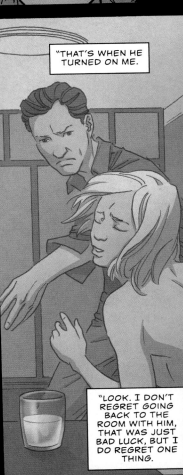

"THAT'S WHEN HE TURNED ON ME.

"LOOK. I DON'T REGRET GOING BACK TO THE ROOM WITH HIM, THAT WAS JUST BAD LUCK, BUT I DO REGRET ONE THING.

"THERE WAS A GLASS OF WATER ON THE NIGHT TABLE. I STARED AT THAT GLASS WHILE HE WAS ATTACKING ME."

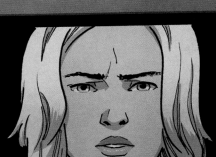

I REGRET THAT I DIDN'T SMASH THAT GLASS AND SLIT HIS THROAT WITH A PIECE OF IT.

ADMITTEDLY LAUTREC HAS GROWN ON ME, ESPECIALLY AFTER THAT FANTASTIC SHOW AT THE MET A FEW YEARS BACK.
OH MY GOD, I *LOVED* THAT SHOW. I WAS AWAY AT COLLEGE, BUT I CAME INTO THE CITY JUST TO SEE IT.
I HAVE TO SAY, ASHLEY, MY WIFE AND I WERE *EXTREMELY* IMPRESSED WITH YOU WHEN WE MET AT SOTHEBY'S. I SAID TO MY WIFE AFTERWARDS, 'THAT GIRL HAS SOMETHING SPECIAL. SHE'S GOING TO BE A BIG DEAL SOMEDAY.'
THANK YOU. THAT MEANS *A LOT* COMING FROM YOU.
SO CAN YOU TELL ME A BIT MORE ABOUT YOUR CLIENT LIST? I MEAN, WHO EXACTLY DO YOU REPRESENT?
I CAN DO BETTER THAN THAT. I'M HAVING A ZOOM MEETING UPSTAIRS IN TEN MINUTES WITH ONE OF MY MOST PROMISING YOUNG ARTISTS, *JULIEN BRUMENT*. HE'S A FANTASTIC ABSTRACT PAINTER WHO'S BEEN EXPLODING IN PARIS. I'D BE HAPPY TO MAKE AN INTRODUCTION.
NOW? UM...I'M NOT SURE.
UP TO YOU, BUT I REALLY THINK YOU TWO WOULD HIT IT OFF. I'VE ALREADY TOLD HIM ABOUT YOU AND HE SEEMED VERY KEEN TO CHAT.
WOW. OKAY, I GUESS I CAN JOIN.
SPLENDID.
OH, AND THANK YOU FOR THE DRINK.
YOU'RE MORE THAN WELCOME

HONESTLY, THE MASK SEEMED LIKE THE BEST PART.

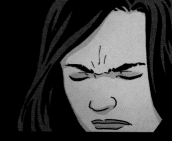

T MADE ME THINK, LIKE, AY THIS IS GONNA JUST ANOTHER CRAZY DATING ORY. WE ALL HAVE CRAZY TING STORIES, RIGHT? I UGHT I'D LAUGH ABOUT LATER WITH MY FRIENDS.

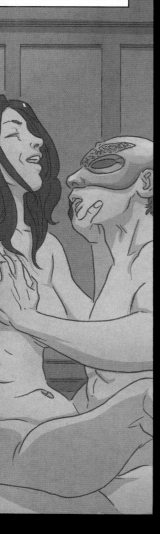

"I HAD NO IDEA HOW LOW MY LIFE COULD GO.

"WHENEVER I THOUGHT I'D HIT ROCK BOTTOM...

"...I'D FIND MYSELF IN A SITUATION I NEVER IMAGINED I'D BE IN.

"THANKS TO MY SISTER AND SOME CLOSE FRIENDS I GOT MY LIFE BACK ON TRACK.

"AND NOW I UNDERSTAND THE *REAL* REASON WHY HE WAS WEARING THAT MASK. IT WASN'T TO HIDE HIS FACE, IT WAS TO SHAME US INTO SILENCE."

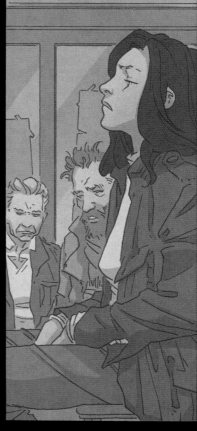

BUT TODAY MY SILENCE OFFICIALLY *ENDS.*

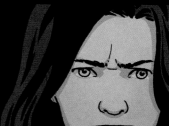

PLEASE, MAKE YOURSELF COMFORTABLE. CAN I GET YOU SOMETHING TO DRINK? WINE, PERHAPS?
THAT'S O-OKAY. ACTUALLY, I THINK I'M FEELING A LITTLE SICK SUDDENLY.
I THINK...I THINK MAYBE I SHOULD GO HOME.
COME, ASHLEY, WHY DON'T YOU SIT DOWN?
JUST RELAX AND MAKE YOURSELF COMFORTABLE, SWEETHEART. WE'LL GET STARTED SOON.
W-WHY... WHY IS *SHE* HERE?
IT'S OKAY, SWEETIE. EVERYTHING'S GOING TO BE OKAY.

STLL HESITANT TO TALK
IT THIS. I MEAN, MY LIFE
BEEN STABLE LATELY, I'M
TING MY SHIT TOGETHER.
DO I REALLY **NEED**
THIS NOW?
BUT JENNIFER RYAN CHANGED MY MIND. IF I'M NOT ALONE IT FEELS, I DON'T KNOW...SAFER.
YOU MADE THE RIGHT DECISION.
DID I?
I MEAN, HE'S STILL OUT THERE. THE FIRM WHERE I WORK NOW ISN'T AWARE OF THE SITUATION. WHAT IF HE STARTS SENDING VIDEOS TO THEM, RUINING MY LIFE ALL OVER AGAIN?
BRRRNNGGG
BRRRRINNGG
RAMIREZ, SEX CRIMES.
OKAY, WE'RE ON IT, THANKS.
SORRY, GOTTA RUN.
WHERE ARE YOU GOING?
I APPRECIATE YOU COMING IN. I'LL KEEP YOU INFORMED.

FOR YOU, DARLING? I'D DO ANYTHING.
TAKE HER NOW, DARLING. TAKE HER.
KRA!
BOTH OF YOU--ON THE FLOOR NOW! ON THE FLOOR!
THERE'S BEEN A MISTAKE. THIS ISN'T HOW IT SEEMS.
IT'S TRUE. WE'RE ALL HERE CONSENSUALLY.
YEAH, AND I GUESS THAT WAS A CONSENSUAL ROOFIE YOU SLIPPED THAT GIRL TOO, HUH?
I HAVE ABSOLUTELY NO IDEA WHAT YOU'RE REFERRING TO.
I HAVE AN IDEA. WHY DON'T YOU DO YOURSELF A FAVOR, YOU DISGUSTING PIECE OF SHIT...
...AND SHUT THE FUCK UP.

I GOTTA HAND IT TO YOU, THAT WAS SOME GOOD INFO.
MY TEAM CAME THROUGH. WHAT CAN I SAY?
WHO'S THIS TEAM AND WHY AREN'T THEY WORKING FOR US?
HOW'S THE GIRL?
GETTING MEDICAL ATTENTION, BUT SHE'LL BE FINE.
SERIOUSLY, HOW'D YOUR TEAM PULL THIS OFF? HOW'D YOU KNOW THAT THEY'D BE IN THAT ROOM?
THEY HACKED INTO HIS CELL PHONE, AFTER THEY FIGURED OUT THAT HIS REAL NAME IS JEREMY DAVIDSON, WHICH THEY LEARNED AFTER HACKING INTO THE SECURITY AT PER SE AND MATCHING AN IMAGE OF HIM TO A PHOTO ONLINE.
T SIMPLE, ? THESE EOPLE CKERS OR GICIANS?
MAYBE YOU COULD'VE FIGURED IT OUT YOURSELF, BUT THAT WOULD'VE REQUIRED, YOU KNOW, TAKING ON THE CASE.
WHAT CAN I SAY? I OWE YOU A BIG APOLOGY. I DIDN'T KNOW HOW DEEP THIS WENT, BUT I GUESS THAT'S NO EXCUSE--
YOU'RE RIGHT...
...IT'S NO EXCUSE.

TO US!
FOR TAKING DOWN JEREMY AND BROOKE DAVIDSON AND MAKING THE WORLD A LITTLE LESS CREEPY.
I'LL DRINK TO THAT.
WAIT, I NEED TO THANK *SENSEI* SPECIFICALLY.
WHY ME? MATT'S THE ONE WHO PUT IT ALL TOGETHER.
BUT YOU HACKED INTO HIS CELL PHONE. AND IF YOU HADN'T DONE THAT, YOU COULDN'T HAVE BLOCKED THE VIDEO HE TRIED TO SEND TO MY BOSS AND CLIENTS AND I PROBABLY WOULDN'T HAVE GOTTEN MY CAREER BACK. I HAVE NO IDEA HOW I CAN REPAY YOU FOR THAT.
I DO.
I GET INTO TROUBLE, LIKE, WELL, PRETTY MUCH ALL THE TIME...AND I'M ALWAYS UP FOR SOME FREE LEGAL HELP. TRUST ME, YOU'LL HAVE A CHANCE TO REPAY ME, SOONER THAN YOU WANT!
SO HOW'D YOU TWO GET OUT OF THE HOUSE TONIGHT? I MEAN, YOU DIDN'T FORGET ABOUT YOUR KIDS, DID YOU?
MY PARENTS ARE BABYSITTING.
WAIT, SO THIS IS A *DATE NIGHT* FOR YOU TWO? NO WONDER I FEEL LIKE I'VE BEEN HOLDING THE CANDLE.
COME ON... STAY.
NAH, IT'S COOL. I GOT SOME RUSSIANS I NEED TO HACK TONIGHT, ANYHOO. I JUST SWUNG BY FOR A QUICK ONE.

S RIGHT. YOU E PRETTY CREDIBLE.
I DIDN'T HEAR HER SAY THAT.
EN I'M ING IT.
YOU SURE WE'RE OKAY NOW?
YEAH. I MEAN, I THINK IT'S BEST TO TAKE THINGS DAY BY DAY, BUT WE HAVE TO KEEP MOVING AHEAD. NO MORE LOOKING BACK.
I'M ON BOARD FOR THAT.
ST WANT TO PROMISE --RIGHT HERE, RIGHT --THAT I'LL NEVER DO ETHING SO STUPID, SO HOUGHTLESS, EVER AGAIN.
YOU DON'T HAVE TO PROMISE ME ANYTHING.
YES...ACTUALLY I DO.
I CAN'T LIVE LIKE I'M A VICTIM. I MADE A CHOICE TO DO WHAT I DID, AN AWFUL CHOICE. I WASN'T COERCED OR DRUGGED LIKE SOME OF THOSE OTHER WOMEN.
OKAY, THANK GOD YOU WEREN'T A VICTIM IN THAT SENSE...
...BUT YOU DIDN'T ASK TO BE BLACKMAILED, YOU DIDN'T ASK TO BE THREATENED. THOSE PEOPLE ARE PREDATORS, JENNIFER.
I HAVE TO BE HONEST WITH YOU. IF THE SITUATION WERE REVERSED, I DON'T KNOW IF I'D BE ABLE TO FORGIVE YOU.
THEN YOU WOULD'VE MADE AN INCREDIBLE MISTAKE.

YEAH, YOU'RE RIGHT, WE'RE *DEFINITELY* OKAY.
TOO BAD WE HAVE TO GO HOME. I'D LOVE TO SLIP AWAY WITH YOU, CHECK INTO A HOTEL FOR A FEW HOURS, OR BETTER YET, A WHOLE WEEKEND.
I LOVE THAT IDEA, LET'S PLAN THAT--MY PARENTS CAN BABYSIT. BUT YOU HAVE TO PROMISE ONE THING.
ANYTHING.
NO MASKS ALLOWED.
NO WORRIES THERE, I PROMISE...
...I'M THROUGH WITH MASKS.
THE END

LETTERS FROM THE CREATORS OF

CASUAL *Fling*

elcome to *Casual Fling*.

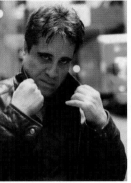
Jason Starr

You may know us from our previous comics for AWA—I wrote *Red Border* and Dalibor was the artist on *Hotell.* If you've read these books, you know that ey're dark, gritty, visceral, and often etty disturbing. *Hotell* fits squarely o the horror genre and *Red Border* a horror/action thriller, and there's enty of violence and scares in both oks. Many of the previous comics 've worked on have, well, not been r the faint of heart. At Marvel, I wrote e entire *Wolverine MAX* series, and Punisher comic also in the MAX iverse, and I'm not even sure how any characters didn't survive those oks. Meanwhile, Dalibor was the tist on a series that literally killed off e entire Marvel universe.

With Dalibor and I teaming up, you might think that *Casual Fling* will be the bloodiest comic of all time, that you'll need a scorecard to keep track of the bodies.

Get ready for the unexpected.

While *Casual Fling* may be as dark as any comic Dalibor and I have ever created, this is a different type of darkness. This is a story about manipulation, betrayal, sex games and revenge. This is about psychological darkness.

I'm a big fan of so-called erotic thrillers, like *Fatal Attraction*, and this book fits squarely into that genre (but with a big present-day twist). It's sexy and fun and has some of my favorite characters I've ever created (including one whom Dalibor and I want to take to another book—you'll figure out who), but writing it did present its challenges. Mainly, how do you create a visual comic that is predominantly about internal darkness?

Thematically, *Casual Fling* may be more similar to some of the noir novels I've written, like *Twisted City*

Their pages create the perfect noir mood for this story, and provide a foreboding sense of doom that looms over every page.

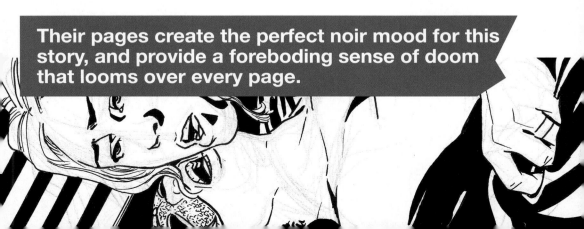

or *Panic Attack*, than my previous comics. But in novels, I can get into my characters' heads with interior monologues; here, I had to come up with visceral ways to show these big emotional moments.

I think Dalibor faced a similar challenge with his art, and you'll see he's done a brilliant job of finding the nuances in this story and bringing the drama to life. This may be some of the most emotional work he's ever done and, yeah, he killed it with the sex scenes too.

The way Marco Lesko's colors complement Dalibor's work, it's hard to believe this is the first time they've worked together. Their combined

pages create the perfect noir mood this story, and provide a forebodi sense of doom that looms over eve page. The covers by Dani are wor of art in their own right. Some I planning to blow up and frame.

So get ready to enter this visu world of psychological darkness, a I hope you have as much fun readi this book as we did creating it.

- Jason St

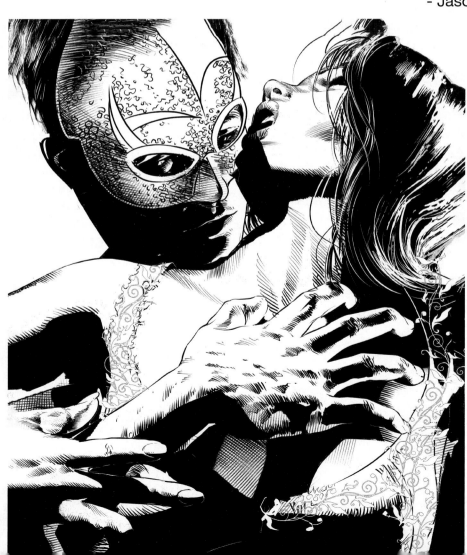

nally, after fifteen years of my ofessional career, a comic book y wife is waiting to read.

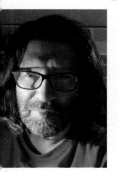
Dalibor Talajić

No superheroes, no aliens, no cities blown to hell...it's a full-scale serious drama in a world of real tangible people so vividly described by Jason. But drama wasn't enough—it

calated very quickly into a nerve-acking thriller. And I'm not just talk-g about the story.

A pandemic hit the world, we all rned the true meaning of the word ckdown," there was no school so I o had to homeschool my son, my her got ill...and I had to grapple h a story I took more personally an I expected to.

always do that. I always "steal" the ory I am to draw. I have to feel it be-e I start drawing it. But this time... was different. My understanding of mance, of marriage, of infidelity, of trayal...let's just say that drawing a slow enough process that I had re than enough time to contem-ite these themes.

don't know how many times I've rassed my wife with my "only pos-le vision" of this story. I don't know w many Zoom meetings with Axel, me and Dulce I had arguing about w to depict the characters and re-

> **My understanding of romance, of marriage, of infidelity, of betrayal... let's just say that drawing is a slow enough process that I had more than enough time to contem-plate these themes.**

lationships described in the script. Hell, poor Jason read a whole 23,540-page script of my remarks, questions, suggestions that I sent to him...

I guess what I'm trying to say is that this was a very important story to me. It had to be exciting, thrilling, attrac-tively visualized. But it was difficult il-lustrating a subject as serious as this one. My job is not to take sides. Not to judge. Not to suggest to the reader to agree with me, or with Jason. What we all wanted more than anything is for you all to understand these char-acters. This one really was a "team effort," in the best sense of the term.

I can only hope that, by the end of this story, you'll see these characters as your friends. As some dear people who made some bad choices, but you are still rooting for them, hop-ing they pull out of the mess they got themselves in.

I know we did. Throughout each and every page...

- Dalibor Talajić

> **I had to grapple with a story I took more personally than I expected to.**

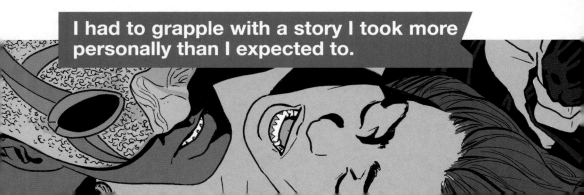

Creating the Covers
Art by Dani

Issue #1

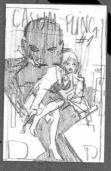
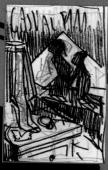
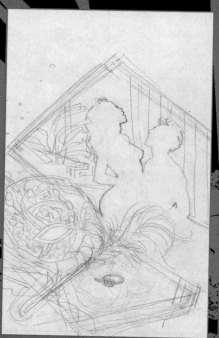
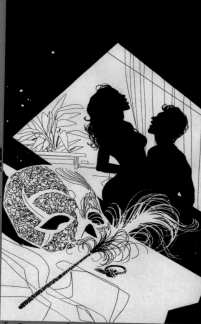

Issue #2

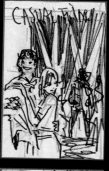
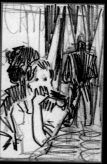
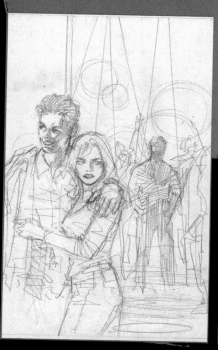
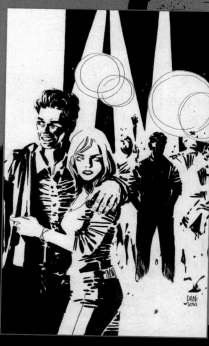

Issue #3

Issue #4

CASUAL FLING

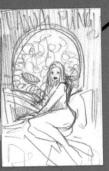

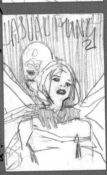

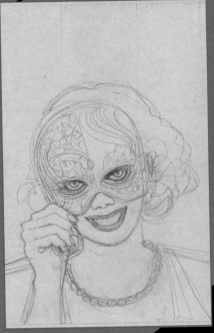

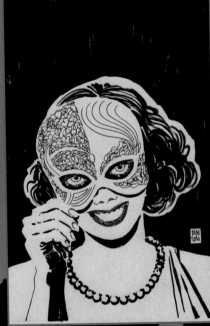

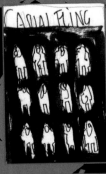

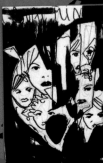

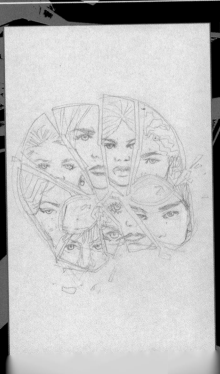

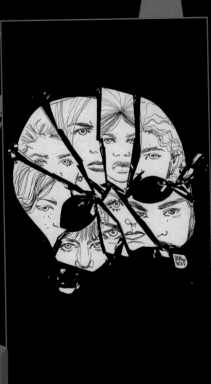

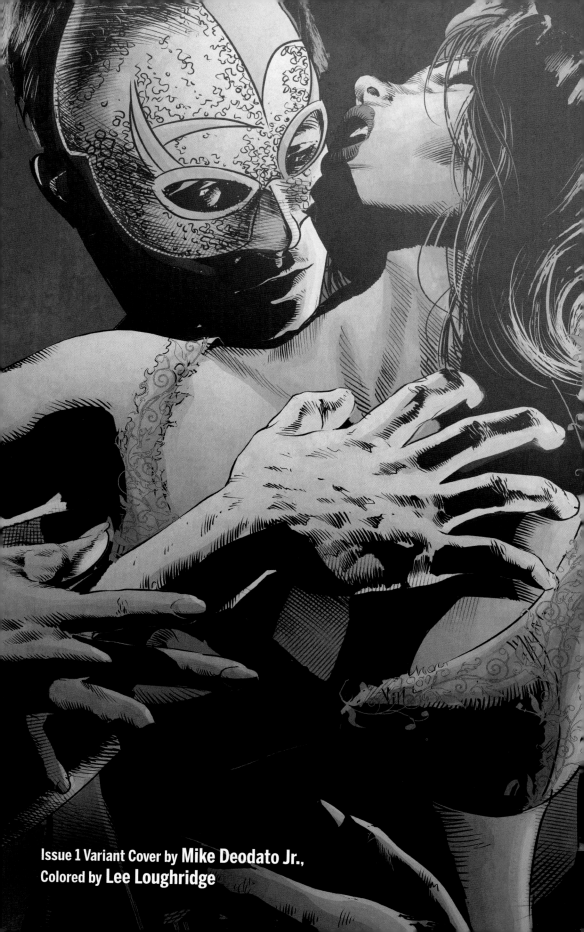

Issue 1 Variant Cover by **Mike Deodato Jr.**,
Colored by **Lee Loughridge**